AF576971

Genius in the Backlands

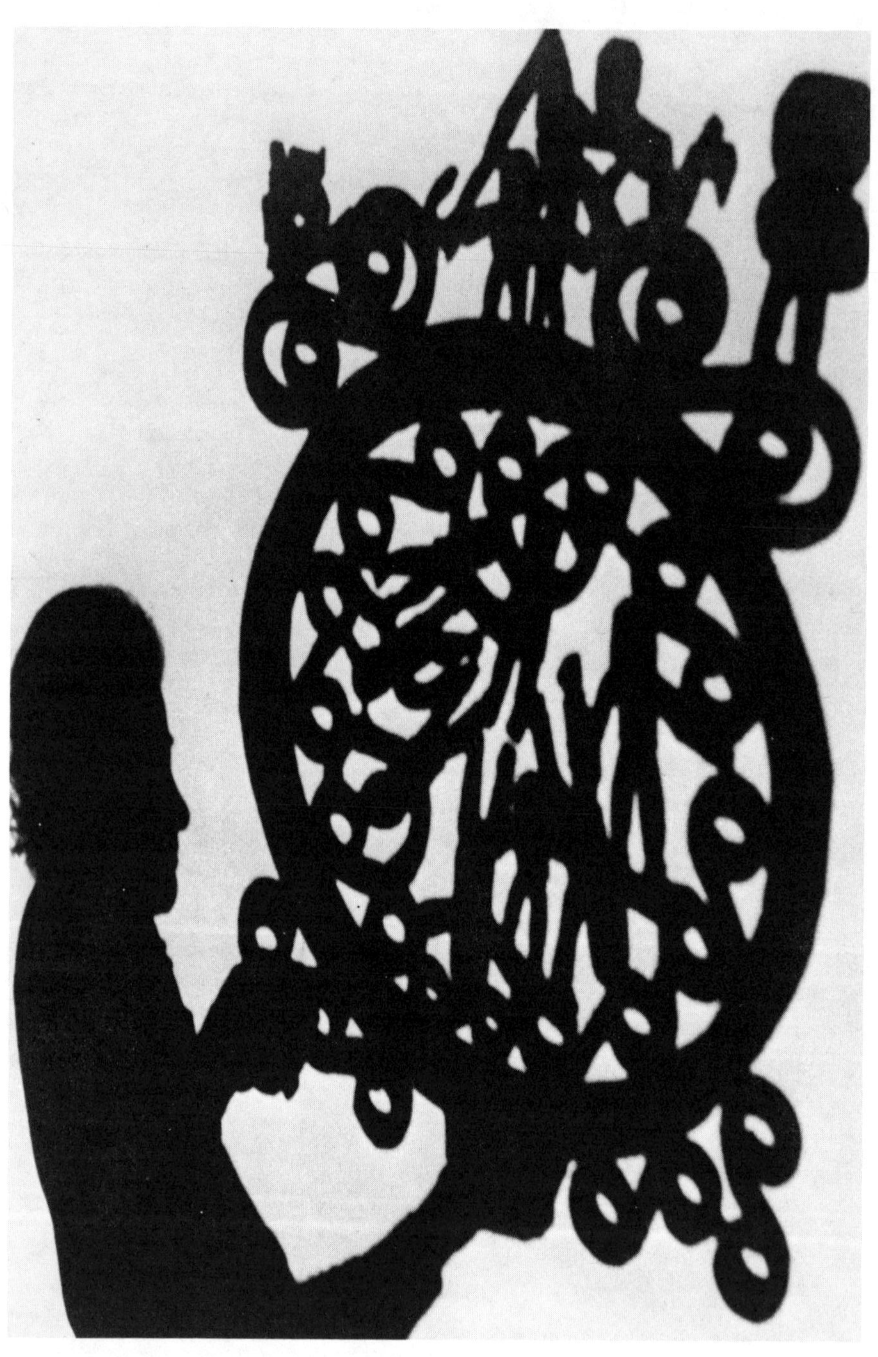

GTO holding one of his Rings. (Silhouette of artist in his home in Divinópolis.) Photo: Author.

Genius in the Backlands

POPULAR ARTISTS OF BRAZIL

Selden Rodman

PHOTOGRAPHS BY
Manu Sassoonian, William Negron and Marilyn Bridges

THE DEVIN-ADAIR COMPANY
Publishers
Old Greenwich, Connecticut

TO
Devin A. Garrity
friend, tennis partner, publisher
who never loses his enthusiasm, curiosity
and faith

For information address The Devin-Adair Company 143 Sound Beach Avenue, Old Greenwich, Conn. 06870.

Library of Congress Catalog Card Number: 76-46181

ISBN 0-8159-5616-9

Printed in the United States of America.

CONTENTS

Books by Selden Rodman

History and Travel

THE BRAZIL TRAVELER
SOUTH AMERICA OF THE POETS
THE CARIBBEAN
THE COLOMBIA TRAVELER
THE MEXICO TRAVELER
THE PERU TRAVELER
THE GUATEMALA TRAVELER
THE ROAD TO PANAMA
QUISQUEYA: A HISTORY OF THE DOMINICAN REPUBLIC
MEXICAN JOURNAL
HAITI: THE BLACK REPUBLIC

Art

GENIUS IN THE BACKLANDS
THE MIRACLE OF HAITIAN ART
THE ARTIST AS A BLACK AMERICAN (with Carole Cleaver)
THE INSIDERS
THE EYE OF MAN
PORTRAIT OF THE ARTIST AS AN AMERICAN
RENAISSANCE IN HAITI
HORACE PIPPIN: A NEGRO ARTIST IN AMERICA

Verse

DEATH OF THE HERO
THE AMAZING YEAR
THE AIRMAN
LAWRENCE: THE LAST CRUSADE
MORTAL TRIUMPH AND OTHER POEMS

Drama

BOLIVAR'S DREAM
HUSTLER OF THE GODS (with Carole Cleaver)
THE REVOLUTIONISTS

Music

THE HEART OF BEETHOVEN

Interviews

TONGUES OF FALLEN ANGELS
CONVERSATIONS WITH ARTISTS

Anthologies

ONE HUNDRED BRITISH POETS
ONE HUNDRED AMERICAN POEMS
ONE HUNDRED MODERN POEMS
WAR AND THE POET (with Richard Eberhart)
THE POETRY OF FLIGHT
A NEW ANTHOLOGY OF MODERN POETRY

Genius in the Backlands

Humanity is being progressively sundered from the physical universe.
—Claude Levi-Strauss

The avant-garde is acceptable because it is essentially reactionary.
—John Simon

When we are no longer children, we are already dead.
—Constantin Brancusi

Part I: BACKGROUND

> *The artist, who in many ways resembles the child, can more easily than others attain to the inner core of things. Here lies the root of great realistic art. The outer shell of the thing, when it is rendered with perfect simplicity, in itself sets off the thing from the realm of the practical and useful, and helps to bring out its inner sound. Henri Rousseau, who may be called the founding father of such a realism, has shown us the way.*
>
> — Wassily Kandinsky, 1912

SEEDBED OF THE COUNTERCULTURE

Every artist seeks to impose order on an unruly world. The great artist, by the depth of that penetration, sometimes forecasts change while the philosopher is still asking why and the scientist explaining how. In the particular anarchy of values reflected by life today, a new art engaged in just such prophetic illuminations is in process of being born outside the faltering Western tradition. Especially in Brazil—so remote save in its seaboard cities from the West, and so close to those pervasive religious cults which are beginning to bring men back to a harmonious relationship with the natural world—is the nature of that new art being revealed.

It has happened before. By all the historic, cultural and aesthetic standards of the Graeco-Roman world in the first centuries after Christ, the great art which we now call Byzantine was beneath contempt. Historically it flouted the traditional styles of Athens, Pergamum, and Rome. Culturally it bypassed the state religion—that routine worship of the Olympian deities inherited from Greece—celebrating instead the popular underground cults (of which Christianity was one) with their mystical symbolism of otherworldliness. Aesthetically the now popular art was regarded by establishment critics in Rome as childlike, naive, disorderly and subversive of good taste. But proponents of this self-taught "primitivism" had their opinions been asked, would no doubt have responded that the art of the declining Empire, bodied forth in the latest frescoes gracing the houses of such posh resorts as Pompeii and Herculaneum, was either formalistic or pornographic, and on all counts the faithful reflection of a decadent society headed for catastrophe.

Parallels with the art world today are so close that only the blindness of those who cannot see them or refuse to admit them is remarkable. Remarkable, that is, if one is so charitable as to assume that today's main-line critics are unaffected by the enormous financial investment dependent upon the orthodoxy of their views.

Since the specific purpose of this book is to examine for the first time one of the major seedbeds of the counterculture in painting and sculpture, this is not the place to explore these parallels in depth. Yet a side-glance at one of them (the architectural one) should serve to make obvious the conflict in values and forms that runs up and down every society today. The conflict is nowhere more dramatically focussed than in Brazil, where the establishment has erected a whole city (Brasîlia, the new capital) to demonstrate the exclusivity of its prerogatives and the "purity" of its forms.

Here, in rectangular *supercuadros* of glass so soul-shrinking in scale and impersonal that even the bureaucrats who are obliged to inhabit them develop paranoid traits, no casual intercourse or creative impulses are possible. Accessible only by private automobile, no walkways are provided for pedestrians; food must be imported; communication is by electronics; and the living quarters of those who provide the labor and services are relegated to rings of "satellite" communities so distant that visitors are unaware that the majority of the capital's inhabitants live in them.[1]

[1]See *The Brazil Traveler* by Selden Rodman, pp. 49, 79-81.

But even this is not enough to satisfy the establishment which is in mortal fear of contamination by the plebs. The popular architecture of the *favelas,* those communities of the poor which have proliferated so naturally in Rio, São Paulo and the other great cities—jerry-built, overlapping, inventive, filled with creative surprises, alive with flowers and the pleasure of community intercourse—is recognized as a threat to the depersonalized technology. So much that bulldozers have been used to level them and "integrate" their hapless habitants in depersonalized apartment blocks miles away from the heart of the city and thus effectively cut off from accessible employment and creative social life.

How much happier the lot of the popular artists, whose works the establishment may attempt to neutralize with patronizing praise or commercial blandishments but dare not bulldoze into oblivion! The pervasive hostility felt for these artists and their works is often hidden behind such epithets as "innocence," "naïveté," "quaintness," or "childlike charm" with which the engaged art of these modern Byzantines is greeted. This self-protecting stance of an affection tempered by amusement was adopted by the critics as far back as that historic moment when the first popular[2] artist emerged.

ROUSSEAU AND THE FIRST POPULAR ARTISTS

It was no accident that the *Douanier* Henri Rousseau's emergence to fame in Paris at the turn of the century coincided with the avant-garde's turning aside in disenchantment from the accepted canons of Western draftsmanship and subject-matter to non-representational styles adapted from aborginal

[2]Since the term "primitive" has become hopelessly compromised by its loose application to at least three dissimilar historic styles, I will use the word "popular" henceforth to distinguish the artists of the counterculture about whom I am writing in this book. I will use the term "aboriginal" to denote those arts of tribal societies entirely isolated from Western culture. And I will designate as "naive" such artists as choose to set aside their sophistication to paint or carve in a style deliberately "popular."

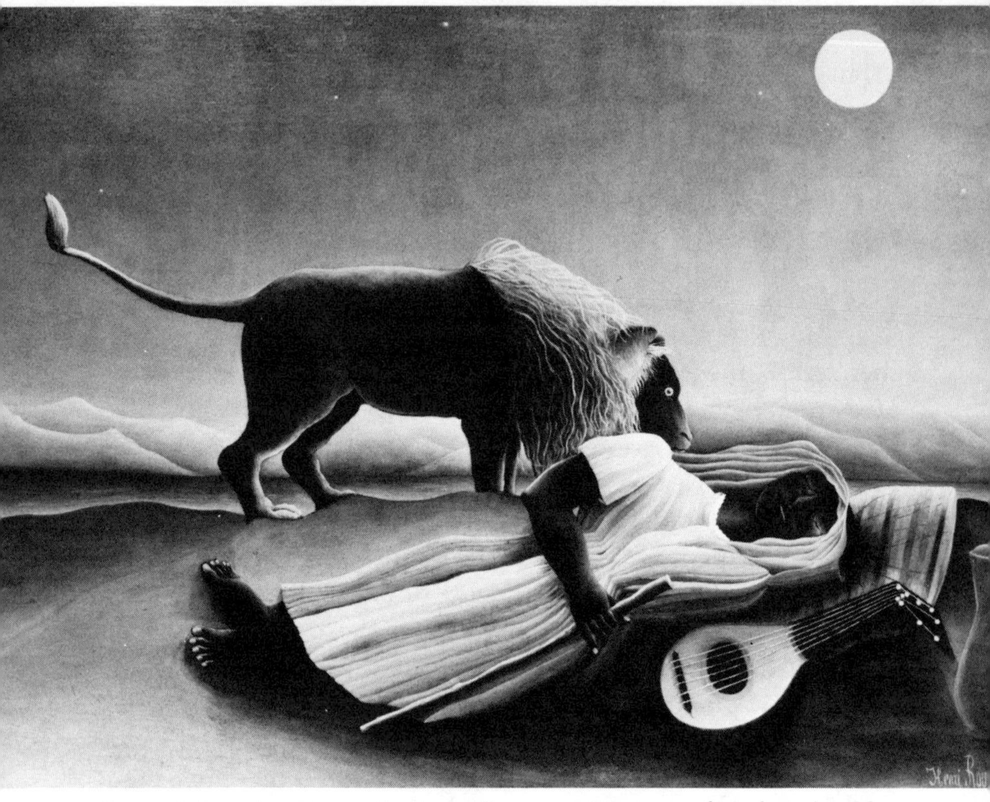

Figure 1. Sleeping Gypsy. By Henri Rousseau. Museum of Modern Art, New York.

fetish-making. It was no accident because the avant-garde, tired of Western art's reliance on the intellect, detected in the *Douanier's* pictures the same trance-like evocation of the subconscious and freedom from realism which they were finding in African and Oceanic tribal styles. The decade beginning in 1897 when Rousseau's revolutionary *Sleeping Gypsy* (Figure 1) was painted, to 1907 when Picasso's picture *Les Demoiselles d'Avignon* ushered in Cubism, saw also the emergence of the coloristic revolution of the Fauves led by Matisse, and the publication of Kandinsky's *The Art of Spiritual Harmony.*[1]

[1]That Kandinsky, the founding father of abstract art and the painter of the first purely nonobjective pictures, should have hailed Rousseau as the "founding father" of a new "realism" (see the quotation at the head of this chapter) testifies not only to the ambivalence of the modernist avant-garde but to the narrow margin by which a popular humanist art was proscribed for the next half century.

This is not to say, of course, that these seminal events in the birth of Modern Art were without precedent—Gauguin's primitivism and Cézanne's effort to reduce nature's forms to the "sphere, the cone and the cylinder" were among many earlier crucial breaks with tradition—or that any of these leaders of the painting avant-garde were affected in any way by Rousseau's example; but simply that the climate favored both the disintegration of the old and the emergence of the new.

As far back as the late 1880's when Rousseau's work was first seen in the Salon des Independents the extraordinary nature of his art was recognized by such artists as Gauguin, Signac, Pisarro and Rodin; it was Toulouse-Lautrec, moreover, who blocked a move to exclude Rousseau from the Salon. But in the next two decades when the *Douanier's* pictures began to attract popular attention, the avant-garde tempered its regard by making fun of the great popular artist's intellectual gaffes and his insistance that he was in truth a sound academician concerned to depict only what he had observed in nature. Jokes in bad taste were played on the credulous old man. Pranksters, masquerading as government officials, howled to see him taken in by the "hommage" they pretended to do him. A playwright with a misplaced sense of humor hung one of his psychologically profound portraits in his private gallery of horrors. The poet Alfred Jarry championed Rousseau because the bourgeoisie was offended by what they considered grotesque in his art, but after commissioning a portrait, Jarry cut the head from the canvas and used it for target practice. It is not recorded what Picasso responded when Rousseau said to him in 1908 "We are the two greatest painters of our epoch," but the remark was prophetic for more than its astute recognition of the Spanish artist, then unknown outside the avant-garde; Rousseau seems to have been well aware that their arts pointed in opposite directions with only their intensities the common factor.

All artists of the first rank share these intensities—their capacity to draw convincingly, to compose memorably, to make images not only never before imagined but instantly recognized

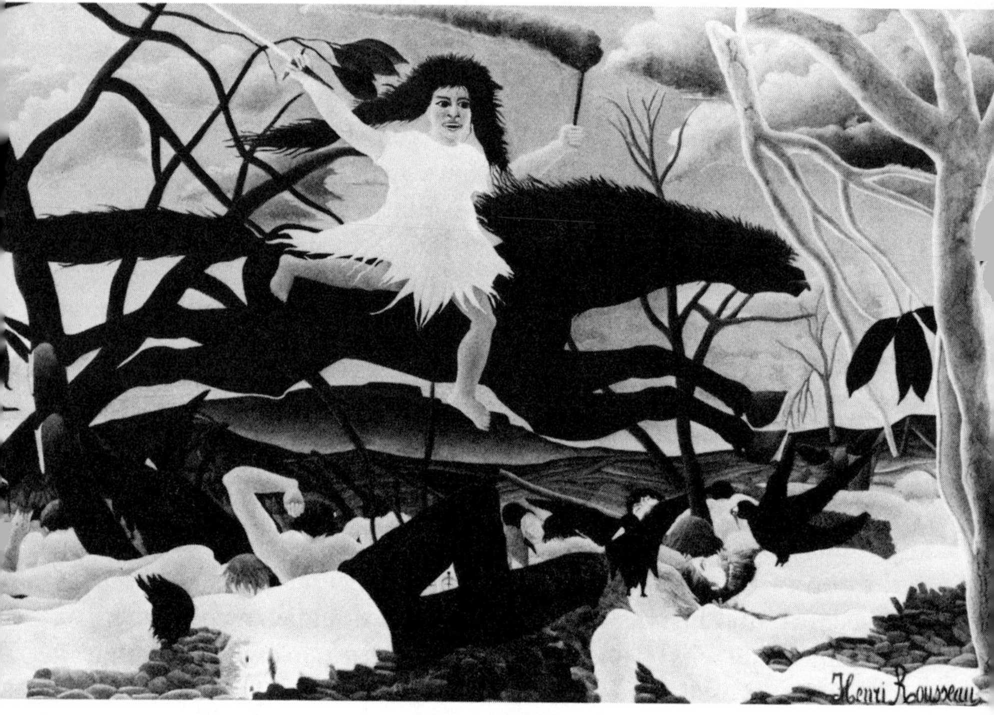

Figure 2. War. By Henri Rousseau. The Louvre, Paris.

as their own—but the great popular artist has an additional characteristic. He is a natural fabulist or storyteller, possessor of that earthiness, that eye for vulgar detail, that ear for gossip, that moral undertone, that makes his work *popular* with simple people as well as intellectuals. Compare Rousseau's large canvas *War* (Figure 2), now in the Louvre, with Picasso's *Guernica*. The Spanish artist's indictment of mass murder came out of a more harrowing and personal experience, and unlike the *Douanier's* picture was intended to influence public opinion. Yet *Guernica* never made a viewer recoil from war and never could: its symbolic components are wholly intellectualized and conveyed in a language comprehensible only after intellectual exegesis. *War*, by contrast, is minatory precisely because it is composed on the fearful ingredients known to all men: the charred landscape, the ruptured trees, the bloodred sky, the corrupting bodies, the vultures with flesh in their beaks; but it is the savage child riding a flying horse, a sword in one hand and a firebrand in the other, that lifts the picture out of banal social commentary: the unconsciously perceived implication that war can make even a child ferocious, that wars are made by children who never grow up, that nature itself when so violated will retaliate with famine, pollution and an environment ultimately uninhabitable.

Artists in other times who have made statements as universal have always been detached enough from the establishment of their time, or in sufficient rebellion against it, to be *popular:* Brueghel in backward, pestilence-ridden Germany; Goya deaf in ravaged Spain; Daumier and the early Van Gogh raging against poverty in the oncoming megalopolis; Orozco aroused by the crimes committed in the name of "revolutionary" governments.

After Rousseau's time, however, one had to be very far removed from the avant-garde's pervasive propaganda to escape the dominant formalism. Or very strong to resist its prestige and financial rewards. Sophisticated artists like Rouault in France and Ben Shahn in the United States resisted these blandishments in their early work. But with a few such exceptions, it was from now on the unschooled artists with deep roots in nature, communal societies or living religions who carried the torch, maligned or urewarded for the most part.

In France, during the early decades of the century and encouraged by Rousseau's unique fame, there were many such painters: André Bauchant, Camille Bombois, Dominique-Paul Peyronnet, Seraphine Louis, Louis Vivin. In the United States, Horace Pippin, Morris Hirshfield, John Kane and the sculptor William Edmondson, were as outstanding. In Yugoslavia, where folk art persisted in remote villages after it had disappeared in most of the rest of Western Europe, Slavic peasants in Hlebine and Šumadija established "schools" of popular painting under the supervision of such teluric talents as Ivan Generalić and Janko Brašić.

THE HAITIAN EXPERIENCE

In Haiti a more astonishing development occurred in the 1940's. This small Caribbean nation populated by the descendants of slaves imported from Africa by the French in the 18th Century had never seen a presentable painting or sculpture in the hundred and fifty years of its existence. Suddenly it erupted with plastic creativity. A score of artists, each an original, appeared out of nowhere; and among them several of genius: Georges Liautaud, who cut and balanced metal as inventively as Calder but more profoundly (Figure 3); Hector Hyppolite, André Pierre (Figure 4) and Gerard Paul, acolytes of the *vaudou* religion who honored their African gods with as much richness of imagery as the early Christians; Rigaud Benoit and Philomé Obin who seemed as familiar with intricate arts of historical and Christian illumination as if they had stepped from the Middle Ages (Figure 5).

What had happened in Haiti? The natural spontaneity which is in every child before "civilization" suppresses it was awaiting only the encouragement of opportunity to burst into the open. The founding of an art center provided a market place. A living religion gave ancient myths contemporary meaning. A cathedral's bare walls beckoned until blazoned with such a glory of Christian pageantry as had not been seen since the Quattrocento.[1]

BRAZIL: HEITOR DOS PRAZERES

And Brazil? Brazil was still so remote from the trade routes familiar to travelling art critics, and so huge in its unexplored regions and teeming cities, that when the European savant Bihalji-Merin devoted his massive monograph[2] to the work of *all*

[1]See *The Miracle of Haitian Art* by Selden Rodman, New York: Doubleday & Co., 1974.

[2]*Modern Primitives: Masters of Naïve Painting* by Oto Bihalji-Merin, New York: Harry N. Abrams, Inc., 1959.

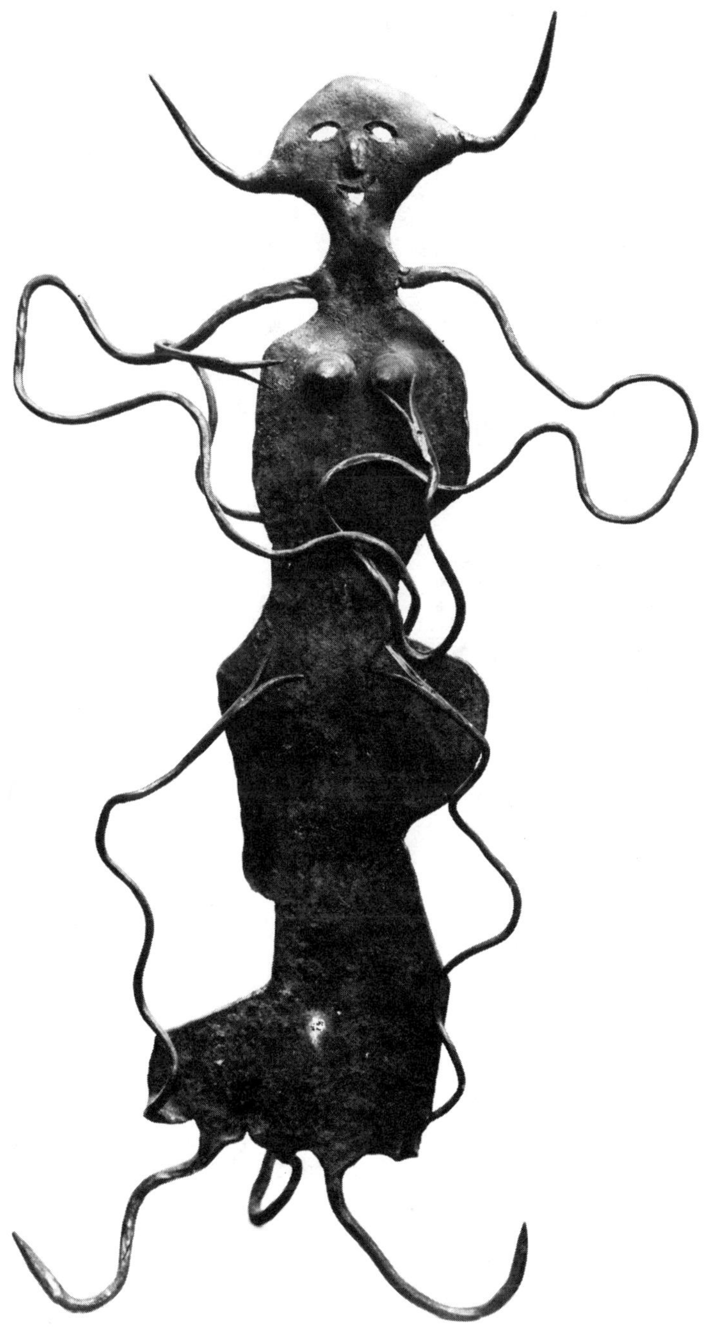

Figure 3. Serpent Loa. (Aida Wedo.) By Georges Liautaud. Musée de l'Art Haïtien, Port-au-Prince, Haiti. Photo: William Grigsby.

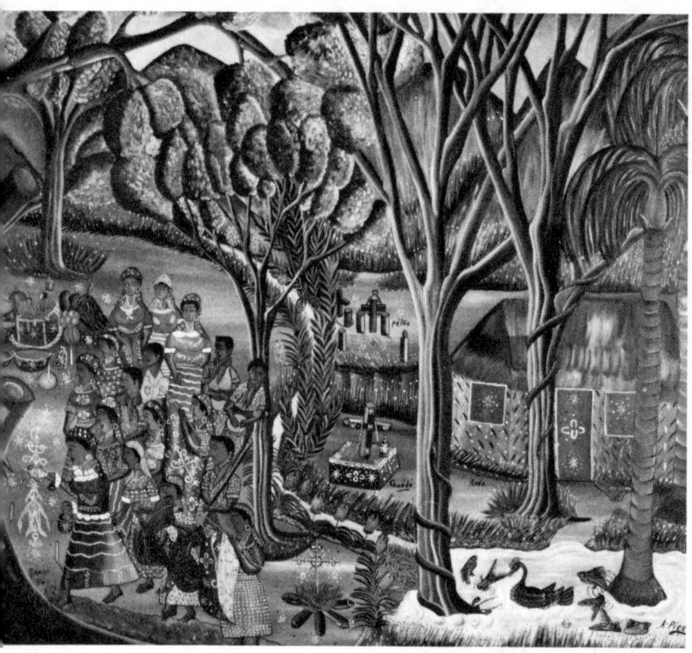

Figure 4. Ceremony for Maît
Grand Bois. By André Pierr
Collection: Author.

Figure 5. (below) Abraha
Sacrificing Isaac. By Philon
Obin. Collection: Fortu
Bogat, Port-au-Prince, Hait

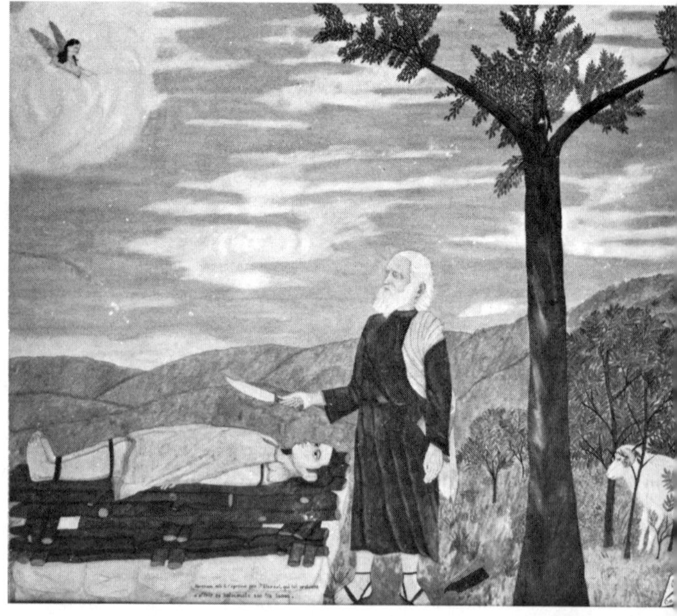

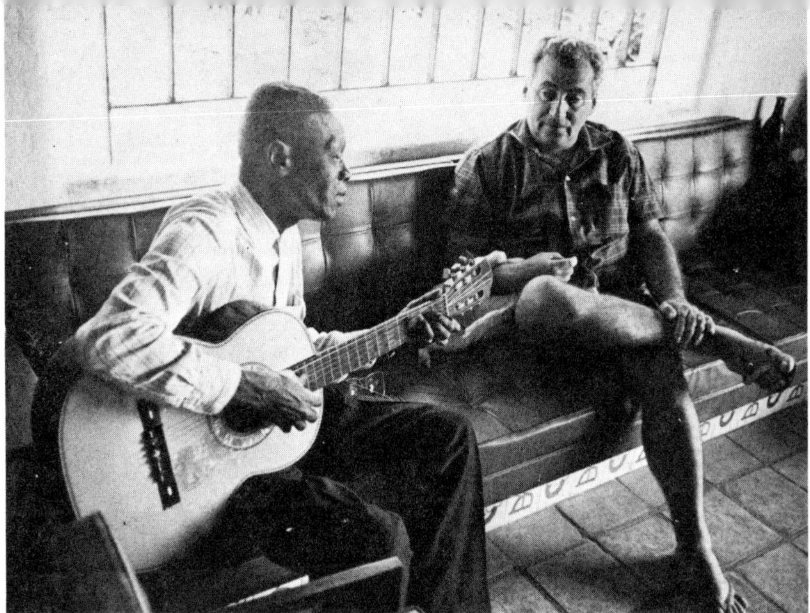

Figure 6. Heitor Dos Prazeres with Jorge Amado. Courtesy Dos Prazeres family, Rio de Janeiro.

the "Masters of Naïve Painting," he included not one word about the most numerous and variegated of the lot, the Brazilians!

Popular art received its grudging quota of recognition, nevertheless, at about the same time in Brazil as elsewhere. Almost coincident with the Museum of Modern Art's pioneering assemblage of popular painters in New York,[1] the first pictures by Heitor Dos Prazeres, Djanira and José Antônio da Silva were beginning to attract some attention in Brazil. Rousseau's work was already famous enough to give Brazil's first collectors the feeling that it might be prudent to include a "primitive" of local origin.

Heitor Dos Prazeres qualified very well indeed. Like the *Douanier*, he composed music and poems when he wasn't painting, played an instrument (the guitar in his case), and amused his acquaintances with an earthy sense of humor. Among his friends, as in Rousseau's case, were the leading poets and novelists of the day (Figure 6), but no artists—the Brazilian

[1]*Masters of Popular Painting: Modern Primitives of Europe and America.* The Museum of Modern Art: New York, 1938. "The painters who concern us in this exhibition…did not know that when they began to paint they joined the brotherhood of Giotto and Delacroix, Tintoretto and Cézanne." (Preface)

avant-garde contained no painters with the self-assurance of a Gauguin or a Picasso, but the poets and novelists were still close enough to the people to recognize a kindred spirit in the *carioca* Samba-composer (Figure 7).

What gave Dos Prazeres' pictures their vitality was this artist's deep involvement in the still-rich community life of the Rio slums *(favelas)*. Participants in Carnival and other street festivals had expressed their creativity not only in the words and music of the Samba but in the making of costumes and masks that had yet to be standardized by the requirements of the tourist industry. To what extent Dos Prazeres participated in *macumba,* the Afro-Brazilian cult religion most generally practiced in Rio, is not clear. But as a Brazilian of African ancestry he was surely familiar with its rites. On the whole, though, Dos Prazeres' art, like Pippin's (which it resembles to a startling degree) and Philomé Obin's, was less concerned with interpreting religions or myths than with documenting the life around him. In this he succeeded brilliantly. His pictures remain the most vivid record of *carioca* customs and appearances in the first four decades of this century. When Dos Prazeres unexpectedly was given a prize at the 1951 São Paulo Bienal his art was no longer regarded (at least by critics familiar with the art of Rousseau and Pippin) as "crude" and "comical," yet his disdain for perspective and modelling continued to offend the art establishment so that by the time of his death in 1966 this pioneer had been all but forgotten.

Since subsequent chapters will be devoted to their art, the entirely different temperaments and development of Djanira and José Antônio da Silva will not be discussed here. But something should be said about the state of the arts in general during the centuries of the Portuguese Colony, the Empire, and the Republic.

ALEIJADINHO

The one major artist to appear during the 428 years from the discovery of Brazil in 1500 to the so-called "Week of Modern

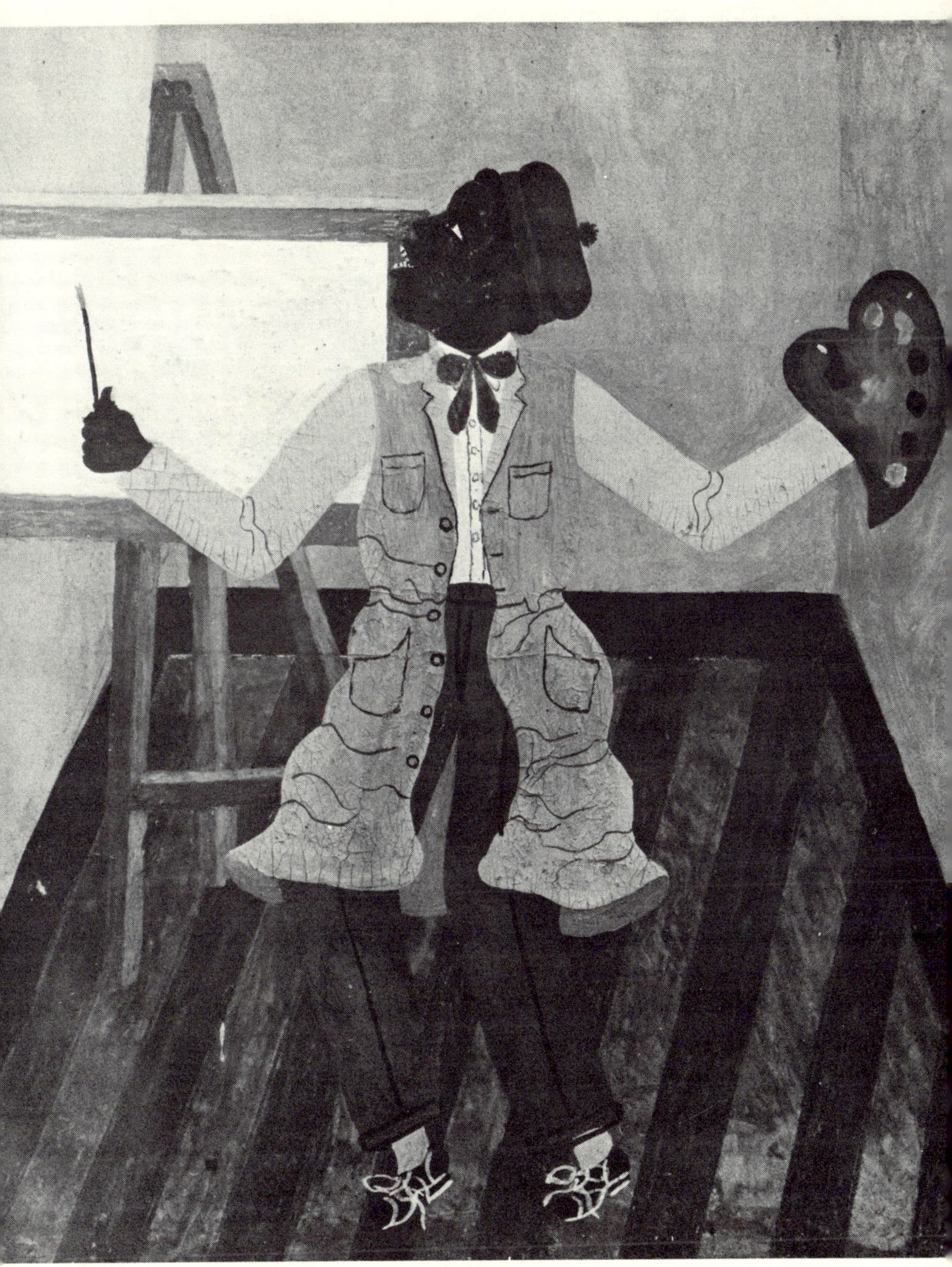

Figure 7. Self-Portrait. By Heitor Dos Prazeres. Private Collection, Rio de Janeiro.

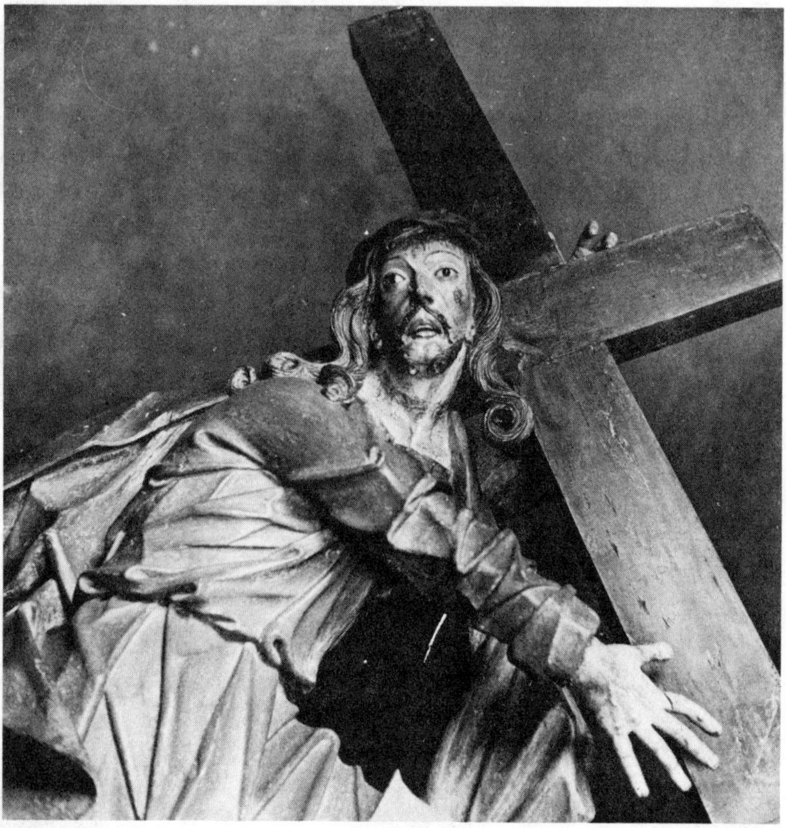

Figure 8. Christ Bearing Cross, & Dwarf at Foot of Cross. By Aleijadinho. Congonhas da Campo.

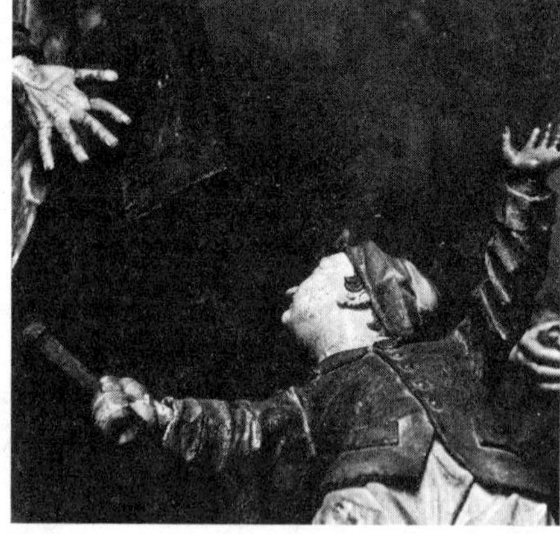

Art" in São Paulo (1922) that ushered in modernism was Antônio Francisco Lisboa (1738-1814) call Aleijadinho, the Little Cripple. Whether this freed mulatto slave from Minas Gerais was a sophisticated sculptor of unusual sensitivity working inside the provincial baroque tradition, or a true popular artist who worked in that tradition of church embellishment because there was no other outlet for his genius, is a matter of opinion — or definition. In any event, Aleijadinho began to work in a style of craftsmen-carvers who had turned out Catholic ikons for generations without creating anything in any way personal. Though his local fame became great in his lifetime, not enough is known about Aleijadinho's personality to determine what motivated his successful search for a style. Was his nature quickened by the cult religion in which his black mother must have participated during her childhood, and perhaps during his? Did Aleijadinho feel enough resentment toward his white Portuguese masters to make him a rebel—at least to the extent of spurning their routine interpretations of the official religion? Did the agonizing pains he suffered from leprosy in his last years—he had to be rolled to the sculpture with a chisel strapped to the stump of an arm—give him insights into suffering comparable to Beethoven's when that composer was similarly isolated from the world by deafness and other afflictions in his last years? Whatever the causes, the sculptures of Aleijadinho's final period —the soapstone "Prophets" and polychromed "Stations of the Cross" at Congonhas (Figure 8) share a monumental serenity with those terminal works of art as memorable for their wisdom as for their artistry.

Only in this century has Aleijadinho's sculpture aroused any serious interest in Brazil, and only in this decade among connoisseurs abroad. Contemporary art scholarship is beginning to recognize that Aleijadinho's innovative departures from baroque norms were deeply rooted in the once-scorned popular wood-carvings of Minas. One might suggest, with less plausibility perhaps, that the mulatto sculptor was asserting his racial identity in the only way he could. Certainly the daring concave planes with which Aleijadinho handles the drapery in such sculptures as the praying figure at the Museu da Inconfidência in Ouro Prêto and the last works at Congonhas have no precedent in Portuguese art.

THE MODERNIST COUNTEROFFENSIVE

The appreciation of Aleijadinho and of the three popular painters already mentioned dates from the years immediately following the 1922 "Week of Modern Art" in São Paulo. The sudden appearance of a Brazilian avant-garde that followed that liberating event was accompanied at first by a recognition of popular art. Little discrepancy was seen between Dos Prazeres' vividly rendered scenes of urban poverty and Candido Portinari's similar scenes—because there *was* little discrepancy. It was only when the educated son of Italian immigrants in São Paulo was made to feel self-conscious about his cubist and surrealist "betters" in Paris, that Portinari's style began to reflect theirs—and lose its originality. Only when this sense of inferiority vis-à-vis the famous Europeans began to gnaw at all the sophisticated Brazilians did their attitude toward the popular masters change. Instead of feeling an easy companionship with artists of a lower social class whose lack of formal training in no way inhibited them from taking short cuts to the same goals—a pictorial art expressive of the essence of exotic Brazil—the "educated" with their European training or orientation began to flaunt their familiarity with International fashions by being as un-Brazilian as possible. The more abstract—and therefore the less differentiated one from another—the works of these artists became, the more they began to regard the engaged and locally oriented pictures of the "primitive" masters with a contempt that scarcely disguised their envy. Museums which had once vied with each other in exhibiting and giving prizes to Dos Prazeres and Da Silva, stopped buying their pictures and even hanging them. P. M. Bardi, dean of Brazil's museum curators who heads the Museu de Arte-Assis Chateaubriand in São

Paulo, went so far as to tell me in 1971 that José Antônio da Silva had somehow stopped painting good pictures at the moment (1949) when he (Bardi) had promoted his first exhibit,[1] and that popular art in Brazil, succumbing to "commercialism" (a temptation against which academically trained artists of the avant-garde were presumably immune), "no longer existed."

I encountered an extreme case of this feeling of being threatened by the universality of the "primitives" in my relations with the sculptor Mário Cravo, Jr. I had met Cravo for the first time in Salvador da Bahia in 1969, and had been impressed by two of his current works, a life-size Iemanjá (*candomblé* goddess of the sea) in polychromed wood which hung in the stairwell of novelist Jorge Amado's house in Praia Vermelho, and a larger-than-life image of the rebel backlands leader, Antônio Conselheiro, carved out of a towering tree trunk, which then stood in the courtyard of the local folk-arts museum (Figure 9).

When I returned to Bahia in 1971 I had been thinking about these powerful images, and told Cravo that they gave me the hopeful feeling that modern sculpture in Brazil could be renewing itself at the well-spring of primitivism in much the same way that Brazilian composers and poets were then renewing their arts through *samba* and the rites of *candomblé*. Cravo, who had since turned to making abstractions out of welded metal and was currently engaged in erecting an abstract plastic fountain on Salvador's waterfront that ill-consorted with the colonial buildings on the cliff behind it (Figure 10), received my praise in silence. I had intended to tell him about my growing enthusiasm for the wooden sculptures of Louco (see pp.), a popular artist of Bahia whose carvings I had first seen three years before in the extensive collections of folk sculpture which he and Amado were then putting together, but I decided not to.

[1]I had had a similar experience with Albert Barnes of the Barnes Foundation in Philadelphia in 1946 while working on the first monograph about an American popular artist. Barnes had bought several of Horace Pippin's early pictures at that great black artist's second show in 1940, and had written about his art with superlatives. Yet when I had asked the collector why he had not bought any of the artist's mature work, he insisted that Pippin's fame after 1940 had "commercialized" his art.

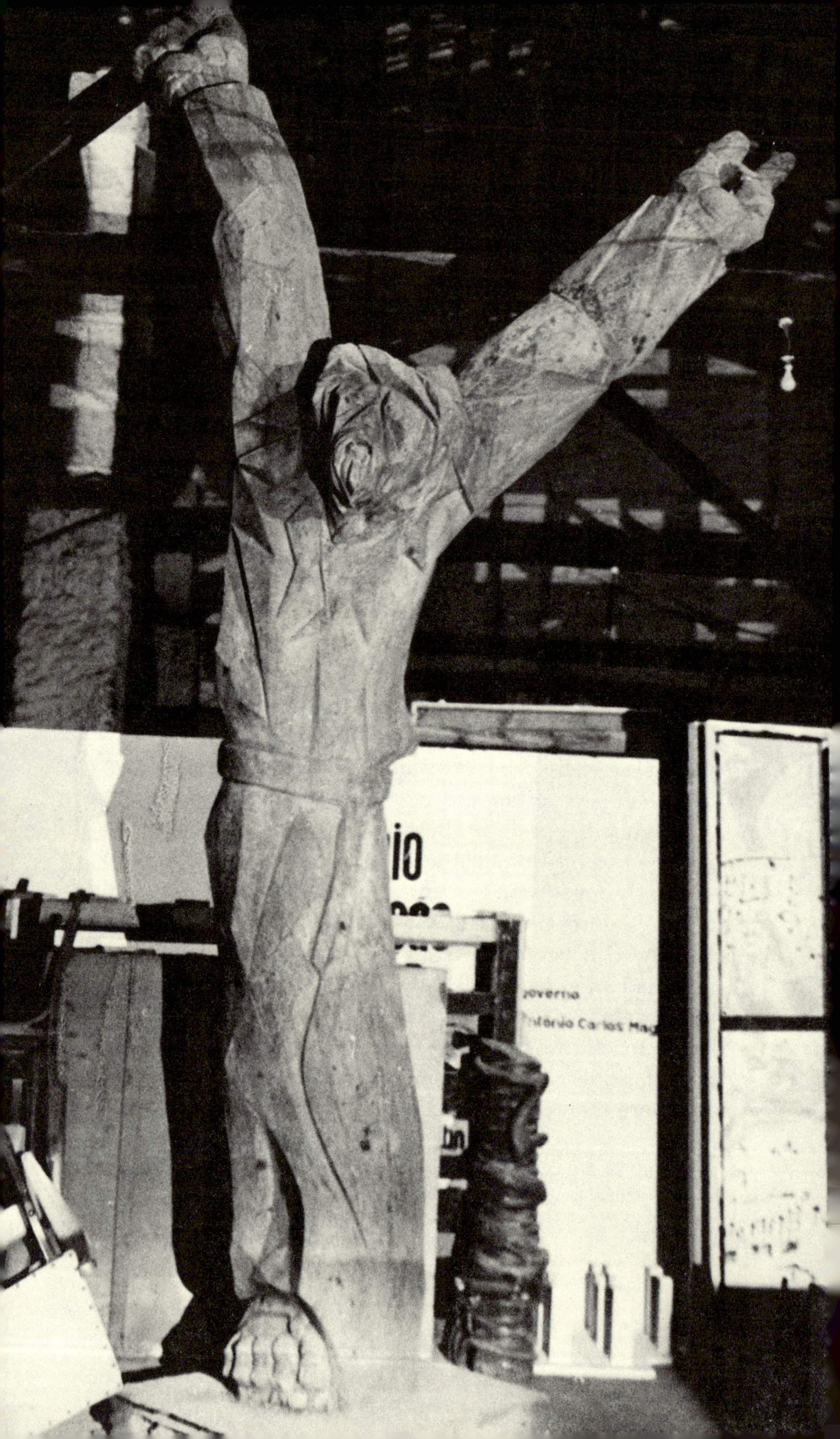
Carlos

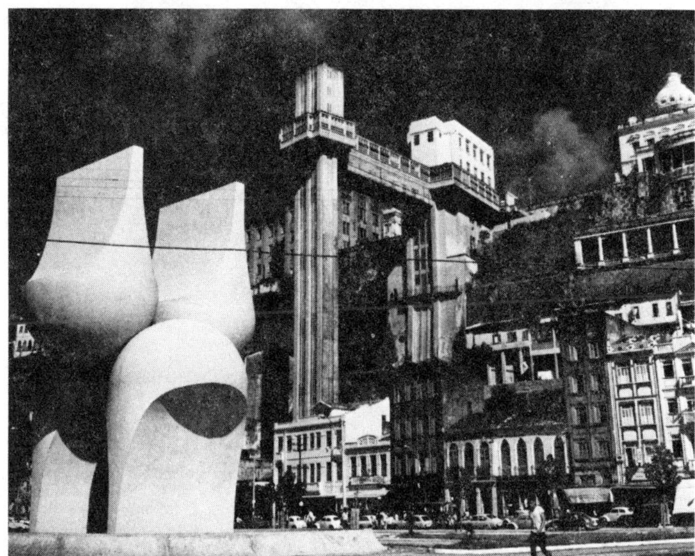

Figure 10. Abstract Fountain, Salvador da Bahia. By Mário Cravo, Jr. Photo: Author.

In 1974, after visiting Louco in Cachoeira and being told that his first pieces had been bought by the well-known modern sculptor, my path crossed Cravo's for the third time. I congratulated him for sharing in Louco's discovery. His reaction was explosive. He had never heard of the great popular sculptor, he insisted! Why, moreover, had I photographed the "Conselheiro" this week in a shed full of bric-a-brac to which he had removed it, hoping it would be forgotten? And why was I always taunting him with the bad dream of these "miserable" early works? As for popular art in general, the angry spokesman for modernism added: "In Brazil it is dead, dead, DEAD!"[1]

[1]According to Amado, who presents him undisguised in his novel *Dona Flor and Her Two Husbands*, Cravo had been flirting with modernism at a time when he supported himself by stealing old images from churches. "Gaunt and heavy-mustached, the much-discussed Cravo spent his time monkeying with old automobile parts, sheets of iron, broken-down machines, twisting and patching up all that mess, attributing artistic worth to the results, to the applause of the two poets and other cognoscenti, unanimous in calling that old iron modern sculpture and in terming the blackguard an innovator in the field of abstract art...We shall merely state for the record that the critics have since acclaimed his work, which has even become the object of study by self-serving foreign journalists."

Figure 9. Antonio Conselheiro. By Mário Cravo, Jr. Salavador da Bahia. Photo: Manu Sassoonian

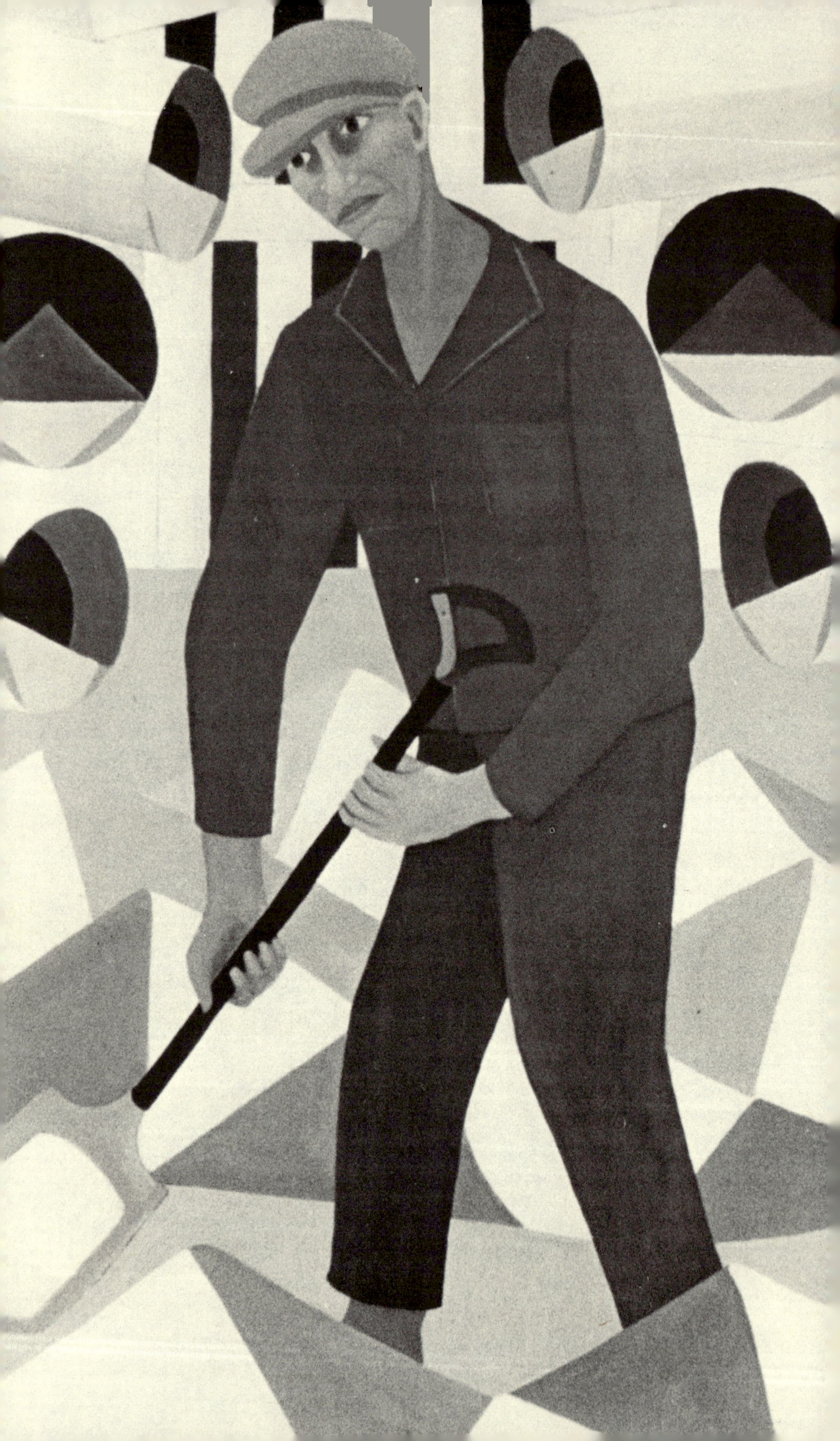

Part II: SIX POPULAR MASTERS

Aesthetes have an aversion to biography.

— Constantin Brancusi

Laughter may express the despair of the condemned better than tears.

— André Malraux

DJANIRA

In all the history of Brazil, Djanira da Mota e Silva is the most famous of painters, and the most successful in terms of financial rewards. She is also a popular artist who has told the press repeatedly that her work is not to be considered in any way "primitive" but rather in the mainstream of modern art (Figure 11). Visiting her for the second time in her beautiful home above imperial Petropolis, I was therefore a little reluctant to tell her about Cravo's pronouncement, fearing that she might confirm it. I had loved Djanira's art at first sight, as I had the artist herself, a woman of infinite charm and sagacity. If she repudiated the work of the other popular artists, I would feel obliged to disagree with her. Our friendship might suffer. But I decided to take the chance...did she agree?

Her answer was instantaneous and unqualified. "If I believed that popular art was dead," she replied, "I would be repudiating art itself. I believe in man. I am an optimist. Artists like Cravo feed on agression; their work is cruel and grandiloquent. A reaction like his is the reaction of a primitive human being."

The road to Samambaia, ever climbing, leads out of Petropolis in the high mountains back of Rio where Dom Pedro II built his

Figure 11. Tile Setter. By Djanira da Mota e Silva. Collection: Artist. Photo: William Negron.

winter palace. To one side is a cemetery with thousands of white sepulchres and tens of thousands of flowers—plastic ones, perhaps, but lifelike in the distance. Many of the corpses lie in tiers of trays along the wall, like miniature apartment blocks—a pleasant place to retire for all time. Back toward Petropolis in a peak-framed cleft reminiscent of the Valle de Mexico from Cuernavaca to Cholula, mosaicked steeple domelets reflect the sun's rays, haze magnifying the layers of mountains to the vanishing point. On both sides of the road, the banks sparkle with pink 'Impatience' which the Brazilians call 'Shameless Maria,' or the tree that flowers with pink blossoms and white ones on the same stem—*'Ipé.'* And the unruly mountain runoffs are tamed as they slide over the black massif by oblong catch-basins, tier on tier.

Then, at a sudden turn in the narrow road, there is a gate in the wall, and behind it the sprawling bungalow with its picture windows of sliding glass overlooking the terraced garden.

The view from the open windows is transcendental. On the horizon piles of rounded black rock look as though they'd been deliberately shaped and juxtaposed by some celestial Brancusi. To the immediate right, a steeply sloping rockface is laced with a veil of spring water descending into a deep pool. The pool is filled with splashing brown and black bodies. In the foreground, lawns surrounded by flowerbeds are more sparsely populated with sunbathers so motionless they seem to be fixtures in the landscape. Directly in front of the open window tiny bottles of sugar-water with "flowers" moulded to pin-point apertures swing from threads in the casement. Hummingbirds vibrate from one bottle to another, the sunlight throwing blue-green sparks off their iridescent, streamlined fuselages.

The view *inside* is as transcendental, and one can only hope that it will be left to Brazil untouched, as a national patrimony. For only here is Djanira's art to be seen in all its dazzling vitality: mountains, jungles and villages; miners with steam drills in their gray tunnels: portraits of peasants and intellectuals; *macumba* rites and *candomblé* queens in billowing white lace;

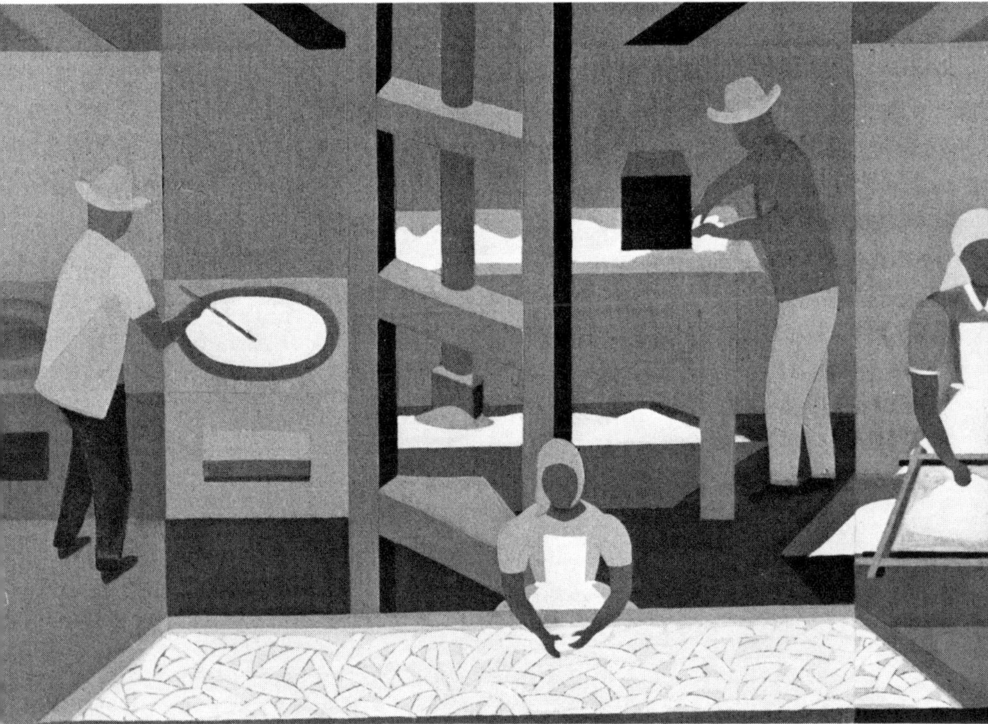

Figure 11A. Manioc Factory. By Djanira da Mota e Silva. Collection: Artist. Photo: Manu Sassoonian.

village factories processing sugar, manoic, (Figure 11A) coffee, or baking roof tiles—all rendered in brilliant primary hues (Color Plates 1B & 1C) and composed with that natural instinct for the "abstract" which all great artists possess and which has misled some critics (and Djanira herself?) into classifying her art with the deliberate abstractionism of the schools of Paris and New York.

She was born sixty-one years ago in a small village in the State of São Paulo. Her father's family descended from Guarani Indians; her mother's came from Trieste, and she was reared by an Austrian grandmother on a coffee plantation in Avaré. She followed her dentist father on his professional rounds. She attended boarding school at Porto União in the State of Santa Catarina. "I saw Luis Carlos Prestes' famous Column of mutinous subalterns pass on it way to the long march north through the backlands. I saw gun fights in the streets. In my family was a revolutionary who had hidden in the attic of a cinema and I carried food to him concealed in my doll. I took odd jobs later on selling vacuum cleaners and sewing machines, and it was while peddling shirts door to door that I met my first husband. He was killed when the Nazis torpedoed the freighter on which he worked, off Rio."

It was to try to forget this tragic experience, and to recover from tuberculosis, first of the many physical afflictions from which she has suffered to this day, that Djanira decided to give up the boarding house she was then running and seek her fortune as an artist in the United States. She had started to paint at 23 when she saw, one day in São José dos Campos, an indifferently depicted Crucifixion and said to herself "I can do better!" One day when a ballerina from abroad exclaimed "You are an artist," Djanira felt her conviction confirmed. In the company of the poet Manoel Bandeira, the young painters Portinari and Segall, and a Roumanian friend of Saul Steinberg, Emeric Marnier, she made her first modest sales. With the money, and a government stipend, she embarked for New York at the end of 1943.

"Those three years in the United States," she told me, "I supported myself entirely by painting. If I needed a loaf of bread, I sold a small drawing. For a bottle of wine I sold a larger drawing. The first critics called me a 'primitive' and that upset me, but after a second look most of them took back that hasty judgement." She regretted the loss of her clippings. "The whole folder vanished. I valued what the critics said *because they didn't know me.* I had no fame then. Who knows what motives those who praise me now have?—fear of being wrong, the desire to please me, to glorify Brazil perhaps—all irrelevant and suspect."

The turning point for Djanira came on May 4, 1946, shortly after a show of her paintings at the Pan American Union arranged by the sculptress Maria Martins, wife of the Brazilian Ambassador in Washington, and on the occasion of an exhibit at

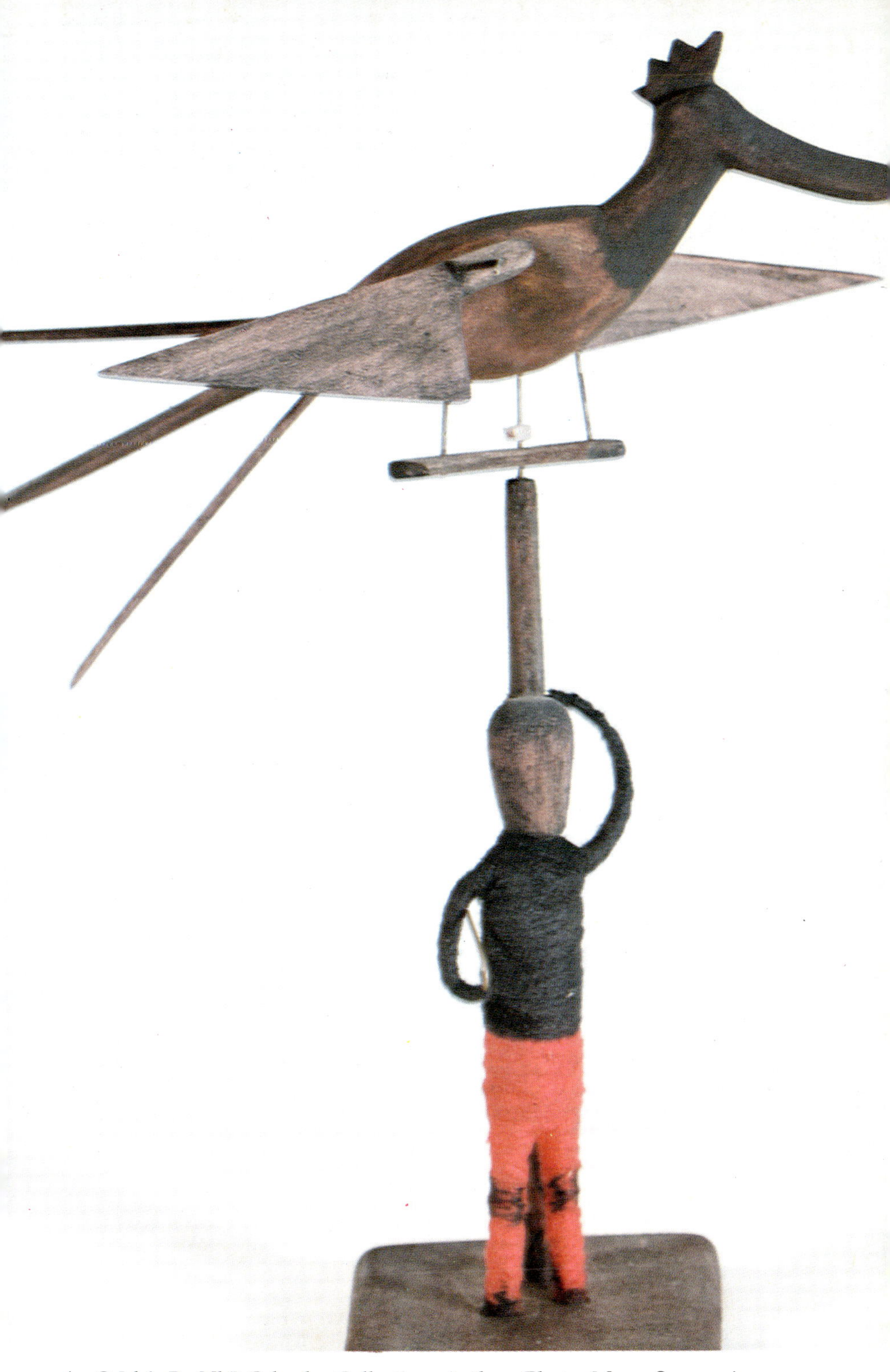

A. *O Jabú*. By Nhõ Caboclo. Collection: Author. Photo: Manu Sassoonian.

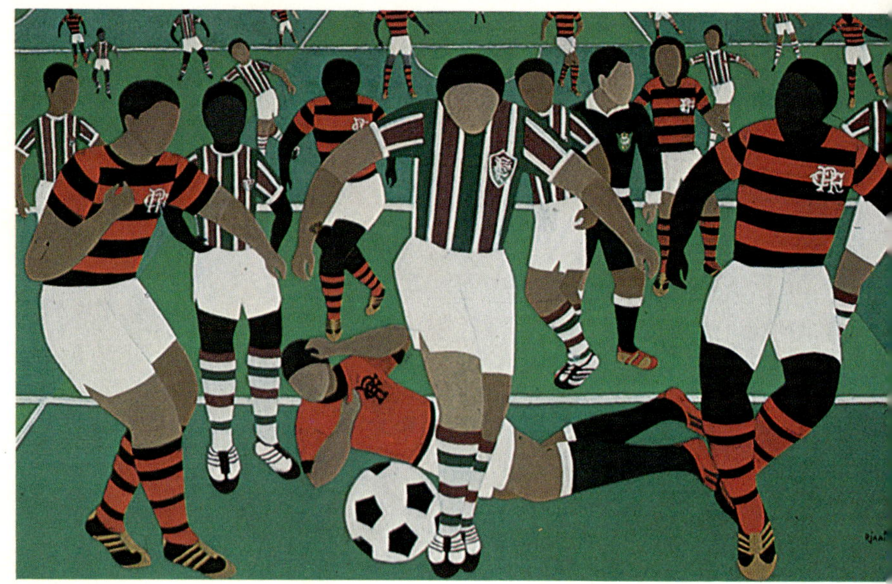

B. Soccer Match. By Djanira da Mota e Silva. Collection: Artist. Photo: William Negron.

C. Mixing the Colors. By Djanira da Mota e Silva. Collection: Artist. Photo: Manu Sassoonian

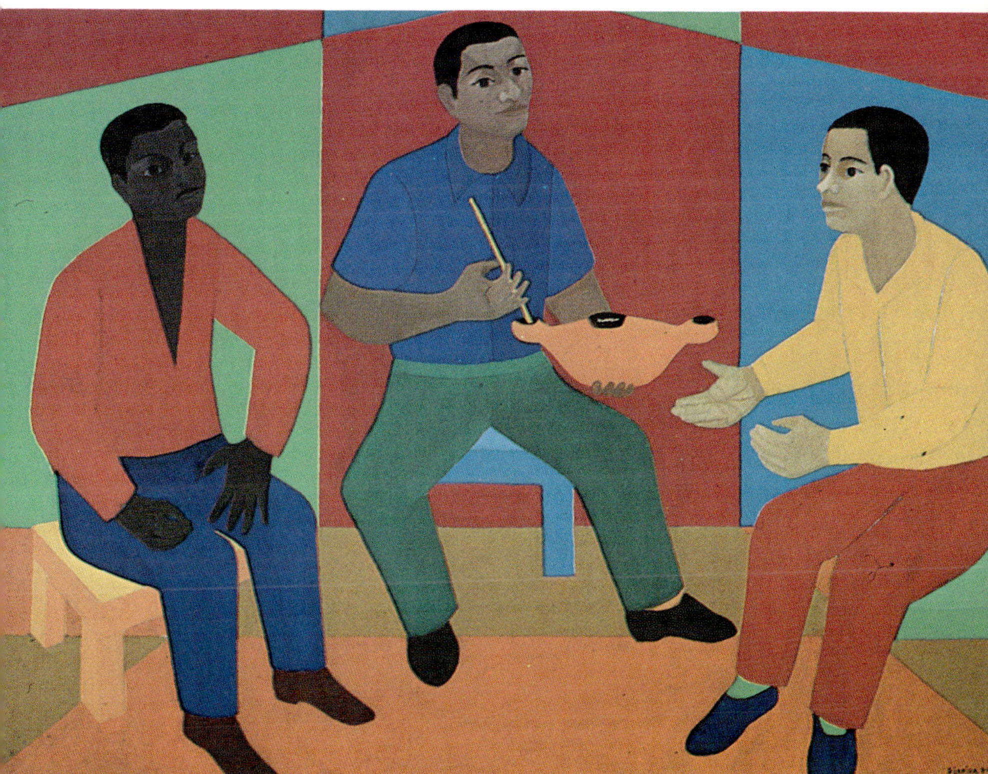

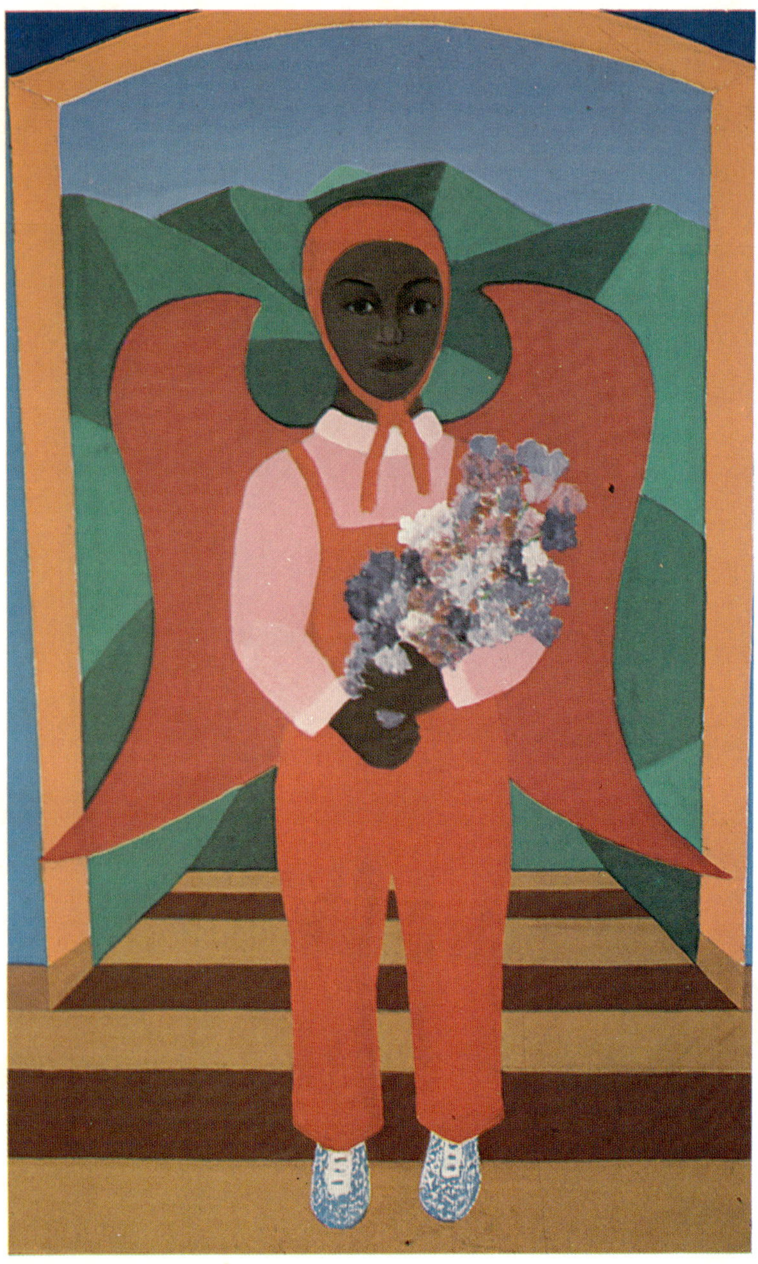

D. Angel in Tennis Shoes. By Djanira da Mota e Silva. Collection: Artist. Photo: William Negron.

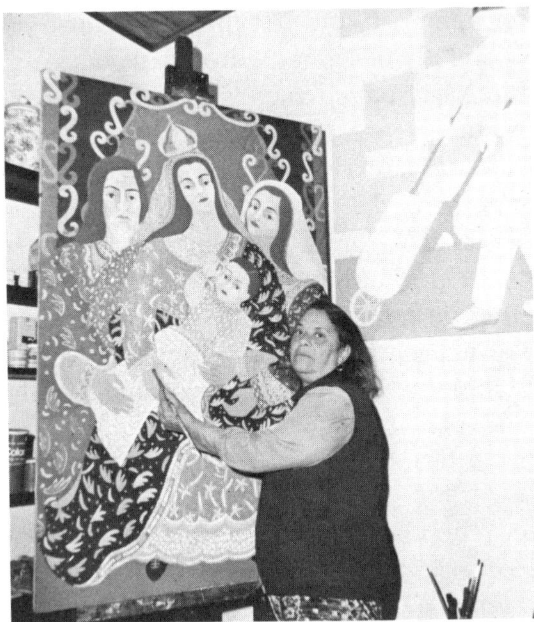

Figure 12. Djanira with *candomblé* canvas on easel, Samambaia. Photo: Manu Sassoonian.

the New School for Social Research. That day, under the heading, BRAZILIAN ARTIST, Eleanor Roosevelt wrote, in her syndicated column, *My Day*:

> Djanira...is only 32, of Indian and Austrian ancestry, self-taught. She paints a world of everyday people and her world has vitality and strength. I am sure these paintings will interest those in our country who are looking for new talent.

Although no art critic, the great lady had an unerring instinct for extraordinary human beings, and no doubt she recognized the honesty of Djanira's observations. When the column was picked up and reprinted all over Brazil, Djanira's reputation in her homeland was made.

Meeting Djanira on the first of two visits to Samambaia (Figure 12), I had the feeling that it was going to be difficult to be objective about her art, and not merely because of the setting which I have already described. She gives off an aura of natural simplicity and *joie de vivre* which is disarming. Not beautiful in any conventional sense, her magnetism is compounded of earthiness, strength of character, and an infectious curiosity about every person, idea and beautiful object she encounters. She has little sense of humor and tends to dismiss (with regret) the work of those few other popular artists whose work she has seen. But when it comes down to defining art as she understands and practises it, her definitions are good for all of them—and wholly at odds with the aesthetic of the establishment she thinks she belongs to:

"Art to be truly international must have its roots in native soil."

I asked her who played the little electric organ in the corner. She hobbled over to it on her cane and struck a chord or two.

"Here's one I composed this morning," and she sang it in a haunting monotone like plainsong:

Carefree
I sing the songs
the birds sing
when the sun comes up.
I sing the
world of light.
Bird songs
I sing.

"Well, Djanira," I said, "you surely won't deny that you're a primitive poet and composer!"

She smiled wryly. "Here's one not written to be sung that I'll include in my next book of poems." It was entitled *Viagem* (A Voyage) and I translated it roughly with her help:

In colors of ivory
I dreamed a wild elephant

from the Indies.
He led me to roads,
dangerous roads
and so far away…

I knew it was wrong
but I travelled in sin
to the Infinite:
losing myself
in Time,
which was sin.

"You told me last year, Djanira, that you'd just joined the Third Order of the Barefoot Carmelites, choosing the name of Teresa of Avila, the Saint of Divine Love. Doesn't that Order regard as sinful the painting of secular pictures—pictures so filled with the sensual imagery of this world?"

"They give me special privileges," she replied, "because I am an artist, and because of my various illnesses." She showed me the huge Y of scars running down both sides of her neck to the center of her chest: incisions in the carotid arteries to forestall an imminent coronary. When I saw her a year earlier she had just had the second of two open-heart surgeries and an operation on her lungs brought about by a descent into the coal mines in Santa Catarina, against doctors' orders, to paint the miners at work in clouds of noxious coal gas (Figure 13). That same year, her husband told me, she had flown into the Amazonian jungle to observe the work in progress on the transcontinental road, setting up her easel and waving imperiously to the bulldozers to stop when she wanted to sketch them where they were.

"Do you believe in an afterlife, Djanira? I mean in survival after death as a conscious spirit, as your *self*?"

"I believe in reincarnation. Not as my present self, but as the same spirit. If Christ could survive, why can't we all?"

"You have courage," I said, "as well as faith."

"Anyone who has faith will find the courage. The courage to

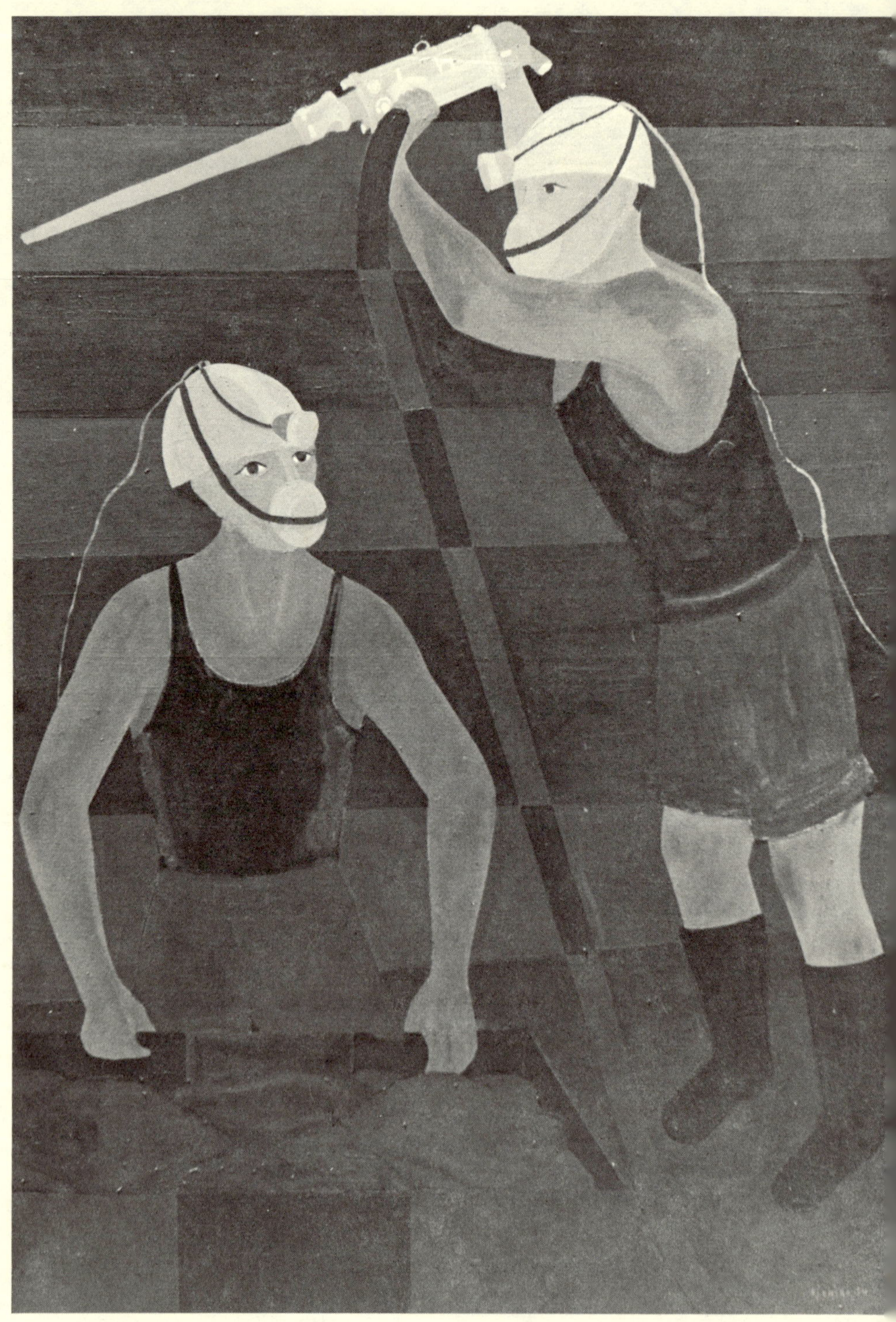

Figure 13. Coal Miners. By Djanira da Mota e Silva. Collection: Artist. Photo: Manu Sassoonian.

survive—and create. But nothing in this world comes easily. You must work, and even fight, for what you can get. God only gives one the tools."

A young Brazilian friend who was with us told us about his early life as a child prodigy, and of how he'd given up playing the piano in disgust over the twelve-hours-a-day practising which playing concerts entailed. "That is the fate of a performer," Djanira said kindly. "If you composed music you would never be tired, and you'd still be playing—for your amusement and ours."

I took a last look at those glowing pictures, so vividly colored, so serenely composed, so quintessentially Brazilian in their idealization of the landscape, the architecture, the occupations, and the people. I thought of the art of our faltering civilization to whose official spokesmen the word that gave life to all these skills—the artist's *humanity*–was the dirtiest epithet in the critics' lexicon. Djanira, for all her indignant denials, retained her humanity—that innocence, that strength-through-joy which the great poets never lose—precisely because she was still a *popular* artist. Wasn't that the source of her strength, of her ability to survive all the fashions? Were she anything less, could she still feel so unabashedly "Brazilian"? Or paint such a gloriously naive image as the little girl in tennis shoes sprouting angels' wings? (Color Plate 1D) Or confess as she did this afternoon that she still rides miles and miles into the countryside trying to discover the secrets of "this nature, these faces, that place"?

"If you love your work," she said as we were leaving, "and only if you love your work, will you be an artist."

NHŌ CABOCLO

Of all the popular artists of Brazil, Manoel Fontoura, an illiterate from the backlands of Pernambuco, is most lacking in those qualities which make Djanira's art acceptable in the salons of the élite. And yet, because this sculptor's work is closest to the "authentic primitivism" of the aboriginals, it is potentially most

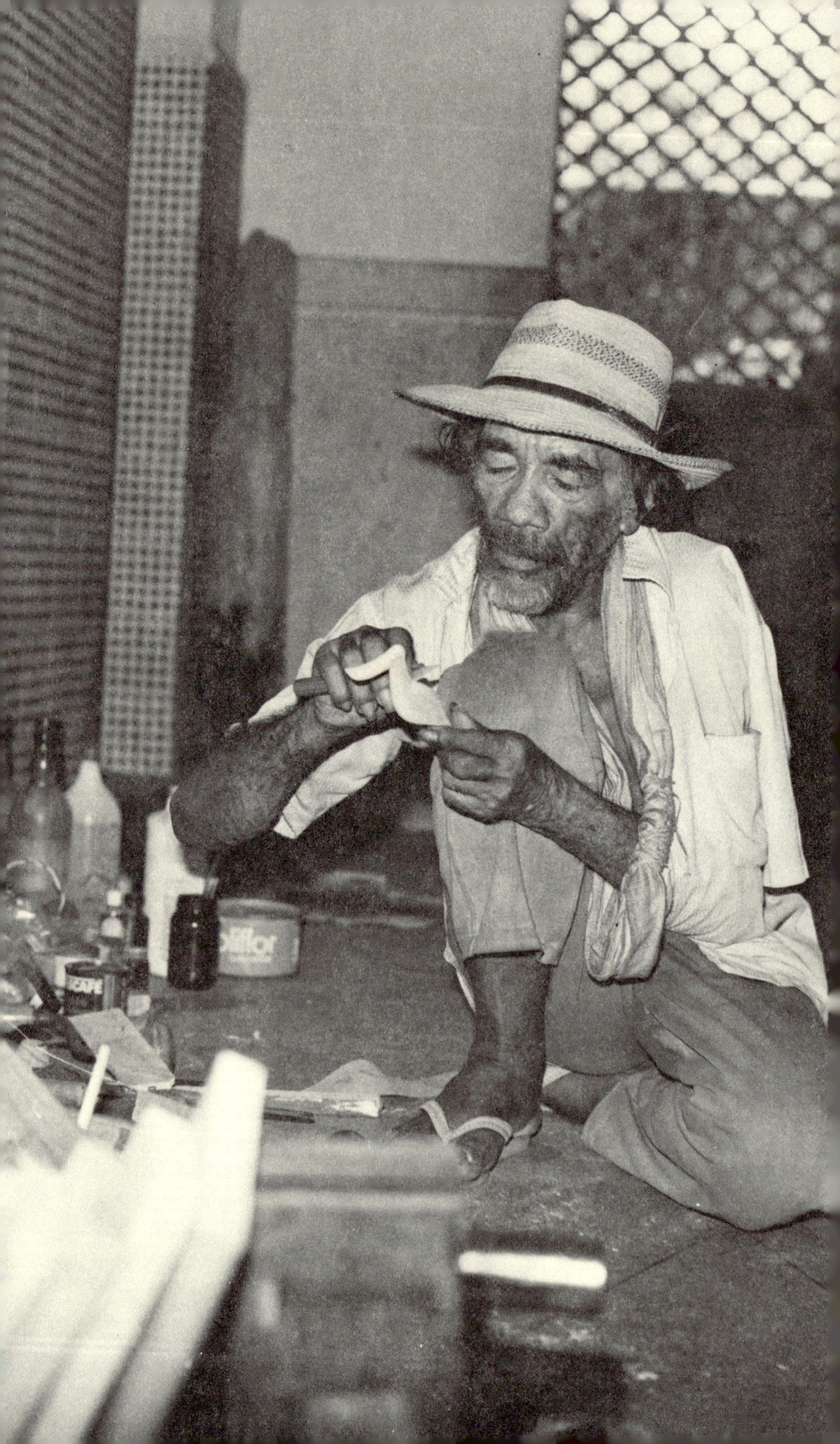

acceptable to the international avant-garde and its knowing collectors. ("Potentially" only because the avant-garde and its knowing collectors have yet to discover him.) For Calder surely, and Picasso if he were still alive, would find in the "mobiles," "stabiles," and constructions of such "found objects" as pipe-cleaners and flivver-fans, the inventions of a blood brother.

Whether the artist gave himself his *nom-de-pinceau,* or whether he acquired it among the *caboclinhas* of Aguas Bellas where he was born some fifty-five years ago, the name means Mr. Caboclo, a *caboclo* being a person of mixed Indian and Portuguese descent. The first time I saw him he was lying asleep in a pile of rags on the floor of an unfurnished building that belonged to the Nega Fulô Gallery in Recife. There I had had my introduction to the sculptor's work the day before: a tiny figure in red and black (Caboclo's austere colors) holding a pole on which had alighted a bird of the Far West of Pernambuco, *O Jabú* (Color Plate 1A).

We aroused the artist gently and he sat up rubbing his eyes. Clothed in rags hardly distinguishable from those he had been sleeping in, one of his arms, deeply scarred from elbow to shoulder, was supported by a dirty sling. He had collided with a car some months before, it seems, and the broken *humerus* had been badly set. It was the reason, he chuckled, that he had no sculpture other than the bird I had bought to show us; he said this with an air of having outwitted his taskmasters. He shook an empty whiskey bottle lying beside him to emphasize his canniness. But then he picked up a small kitchen knife and winked at me as he began whittling another bird out of white balsa. Clearly, though he had a ready-made excuse for goofing off and had no intention of surrendering it, he carved instinctively (Figure 14).

Changed to formal attire—shuffling on a sandal to match the one he'd been sleeping in, and tilting a battered straw hat over one eye—Caboclo started doing the other thing he loves doing best: talking. He is very articulate and laughs at his own sallies. Had he been born, as quoted to the Gallery, "365 years ago"?

Figure 14. Nhõ Caboclo whittling a Bird, Recife. Photo: Manu Sassoonian.

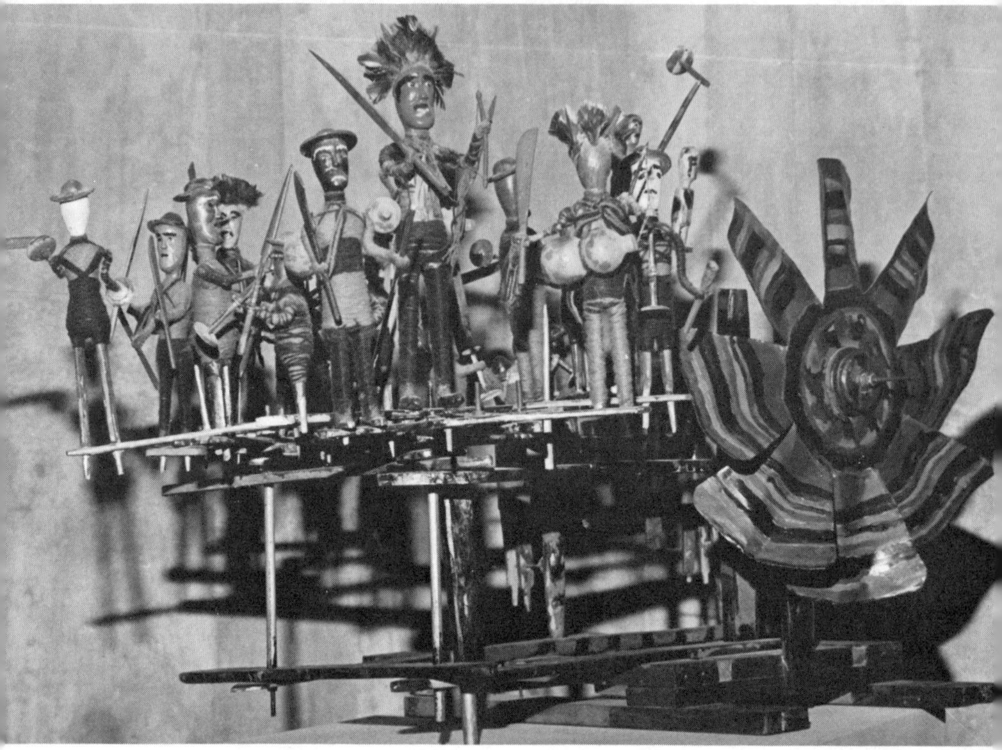

Figure 15. (above) Mobile with Fan. By Nhõ Caboclo. Nega Fulô Gallery, Recife. Photo: Manu Sassoonian.

Figure 16. Counterpoise: Indian. By Nhõ Caboclo. Collection: Lélia Coelho Frota, Rio de Janeiro. Photo: Manu Sassoonian.

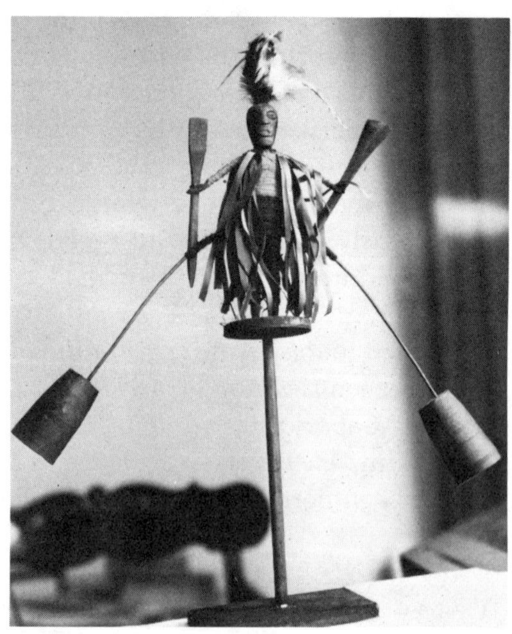

"That was true," he replied, "but they began to take notice of me some 52 years ago in Aguas Bellas."

This village is not far from Caruarú, 240 kilometers inland from Recife, where the famous folk-potter Vitalino baked his ceramic bulls and barnyards until his death recently. The resemblances in the two artists' work are confined only to the miniature scale of their characteristic figurines and the way these are sometimes assembled in occupational groups. I asked Caboclo if he had known the older artist. He had hung around Vitalino's kiln as a boy of nine and ten, he said, and learned a little about woodcarving by watching him. But the woods he elected to use, 'imburna,' 'maça,' 'praíba,' were of his own choosing. "And each piece," he added pridefully, and perhaps in allusion to Vitalino's habit of repeating popular models, "is different from every other."

The delicate bird with wings slotted to catch the wind which I had bought the day before was whittled from *maça* (balsa?), he told me; but the painted figure beneath it was carved from one of the harder woods. So were the multiple figurines of men with saws in pork-pie hats smoking pipes and activated by a fan (Figure 15), which someone had commissioned from the Nega Fulô and which we had photographed there the day before. Where had the sculptor acquired his knowledge of mechanics, his skill in gearing and balancing? Had he, like Calder, studied engineering before his instincts as an artist became dominant? In his case, tinkering with old motors or pumps, perhaps?

He denied it. His principles, he insisted, had been arrived at entirely by experimentation. But surely the old Indian had observed the movements of puppets in circuses that plied the backland circuits, some activated by cranks or simple clockwork. One of his sculptures, a manikin balancing by weighted buckets on a sweep as it rotates on a pin-point pivot (Figure 16) is a folk toy common to all countries. I bought one for a few pennies on the dock at Cap Haïtien, Haiti, the following year, similar even to the little man's feathered headgear, differing only in the Brazilian sculptor's incomparable artistry.

More unique and mysteriously poetic than either these "coun-

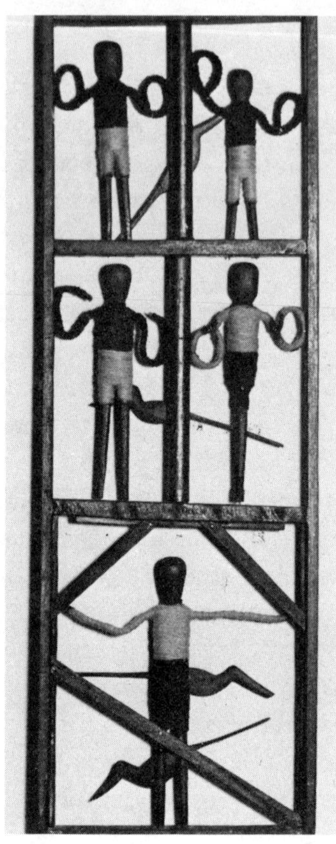

Figure 17. *Racho* in Red and Black. By Nhõ Caboclo. Collection: Author. Photo: Marilyn Bridges.

terpoises" or the complex assemblages of geared figures, are the "stabiles" which Caboclo calls *rachos* ("splits") and which constitute at least half of his output. Wooden frames of space-dividers painted black form the "windows" in which figurines, sometimes painted partly red and with arms of blackened pipe-cleaners, dispute their niches with two-dimensional black birds (Figure 17). Since I had not seen these when I visited the artist in Recife, I was unable to ask him what he had in mind. It is said that he calls these enigmatic *homunculi* "deads": could the birds be their souls? Could Caboclo be exorcizing the demons of the jungle that all Indians must placate?

Sylvia Martins, who discovered Caboclo idling time away in his native village, brought him to Recife. She tries to control the sale and pricing of his sculptures in her gallery, but the artist with as little sense of money as of time sometimes sneaks out with a piece and sells it in the marketplace for a chicken or a bottle of undistilled rum. If Senhora Martins some day publishes the findings of her conversations with Caboclo over the years, more may be known than now about his plastic myth-making.

Caboclo *says* he make sculptures that move because he likes the movies. Why does he like the movies? Because they move! Friends were puzzled over the interminable hours he spent every evening visiting a theater only twelve blocks away, and at the state of exhaustion from which he returned after these solitary bouts with Hollywood. He explained the procedure to me quite logically. "A bus ticket to the cinema costs 15¢ and entitles me to ride another twenty blocks at no extra cost. Naturally I take advantage of this and walk back to the cinema. On the way home, my return ticket gives me almost two miles additional free ride. No, the bus company isn't fooling Nhō Caboclo!"

Roberto Pontual, the lexicographer of Brazilian art, seems to confirm the artist's own interpretation of his fascination with things that move. "There is movement implied in even Vitalino's ceramics though there are no moveable parts," he told me. "These artists put movement in their work because they want to catch life, and life moves." Eliane Lage, another Brazilian friend who once ran a gift shop that handled some of the popular sculptors, guesses that Caboclo's use of red in his sculptures symbolizes evil. "The Catholicism of the Northeast teaches an obsession with evil, personified to uneducated peasants, Indians especially, in devil figures colored red and black. When they gave up the innocence of their jungle paradise for Christianity, they received in return fear and the sense of sin."

Not every Indian sinner, obviously, is as fortunate as Nhō Caboclo in being able to turn his fears into negotiable artistic currency.

JOSÉ ANTÔNIO DA SILVA

The greatest popular painter of Brazil shares with the Indian sculptor two qualities. José Antônio da Silva is as unflaggingly inventive, and his contempt for the opinions of the art establishment is as absolute. But whereas Caboclo's contempt might be ascribed to ignorance and indifference, José Antônio's is an attitude acquired over the years as a result of bitter experience, and cultivated, with the aid of heady drafts of paranoia, into revenge-dramas gloriously apocalyptic.

If it could be said that Caboclo's subject-matter comes out of the dusty attic of the collective subconscious, given visible shape by the toys of itinerant jungle entertainers, José Antônio's imagery reflects one of the world's biggest egos uninhibited by any of the restraints and stratagems that geniuses usually employ to conceal the outrageousness of their visions behind masks of tradition. Thus, for example, that monstrous ego among composers, Richard Wagner, when he wished to skewer the academic critics who had been deriding him for a quarter of a century in the person of François-Antoine Habeneck, created the character of Beckmesser in *Die Meistersinger* with exaggerated pomposities broad enough to stand for the whole tribe. But José Antônio da Silva, when sufficiently stung by the patronizing critics of the São Paulo Bienal to conjure up a hanging appropriate for their crimes, not only included their names in his painting, but even, to make no mistake about it, a collage of their most impudent reviews (Figure 18).

Though perhaps not the first of his expressionist pictures, and certainly not the best, this painting is important symbolically as marking the artist's consciousness of his role as a rebel. The popular "impressionism" of his pictures of the 1940's and early 1950's carried no message, polemical or moral, and offended no one. They coincided with his "discovery" by the critics and collectors of São Paulo, his appearances and awards at the Bienal, and his early fame in Brazil at the time when his art and Dos Prazeres' were accepted by the establishment as a kind of

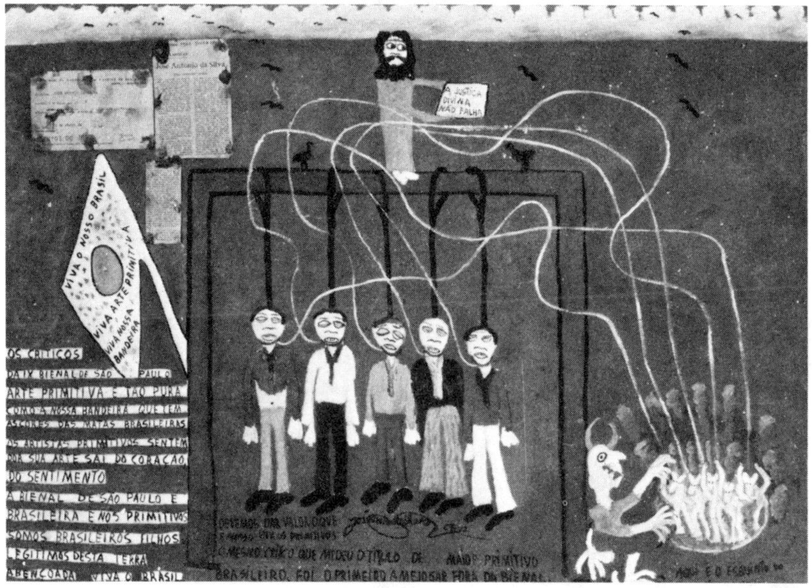

Figure 18. Hanging the Critics. By José Antônio da Silva. Museu, São José do Rio Prêto.

Rousseau-like appendix to the works of the Brazilian avant-garde which had emerged in the wake of the São Paulo "Week of Modern Art" of 1922.

Whether the paintings of this early phase have an "impressionist" look because José Antônio had seen pictures by the French masters of that genre in Assis Chateaubriand's collection and was endeavoring to please his patrons by emulating certain of the Impressionists' techniques and characteristic subjects, or whether the popular painter simply painted that way and was therefore found acceptable because he did, is not important. One of the best of these low-keyed early pictures, "Houses in the Rain" (Color Plate 2A), has a shimmering atmosphere of diffused light that would do credit to the most poetic evocations of a Whistler or a Pisarro, and it is therefore often cited as evidence of the kind of talent José Antônio "once had" before he

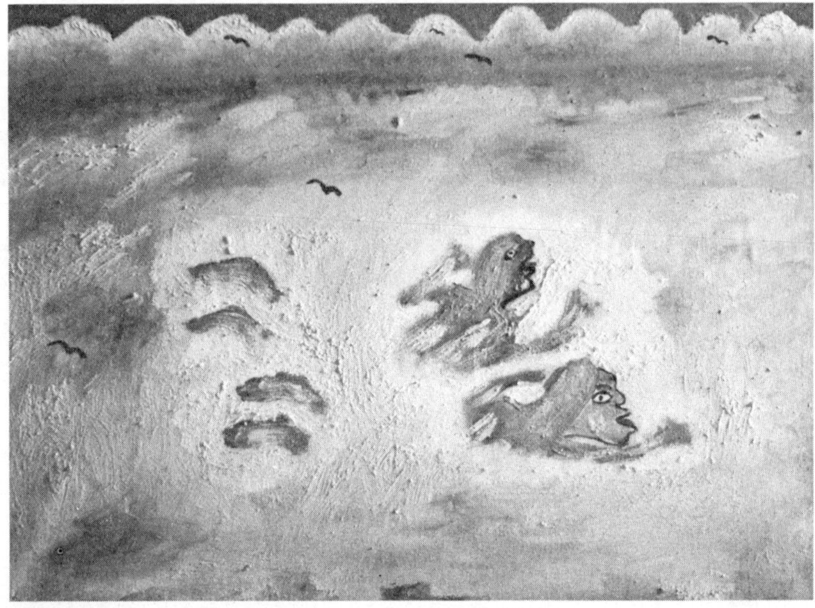

Figure 19. Swimmers. By José Antônio da Silva. Collection: Crisaldo Morais, São Paulo. Photo: Manu Sassoonian.

"went the way of all primitives" and became "crude," "over-ambitious" and "commercialized."

Again, the question of whether José Antônio changed his style from "impressionism" to "expressionism" because he was goaded by the patronizing attitude of his fair-weather friends, or whether he shifted gears the better to express his turbulent temperament and dislocated life, and therefore lost the avant-garde's esteem, matters little. The far more original and ambitious style on which the artist was now embarked offended almost everyone. By the time I made my first visits to Brazil in 1969 and 1971 José Antônio's pictures were to be seen only in a few *déclassé* gift shops in São Paulo, and in the budding private collections of such sophisticated naives and militant friends of the artist as Iraçema Arditi, who then lived in Paris, and Crisaldo Morais.

Pictures from these collections, and the artist's own hoard, illustrate very well the radical turn his *oeuvre* had now taken. Least shocking were those like the two I have called "Roundup" and "Demon Stampeding the Herd" (Color Plates 2B1 & 2B2) in which José Antônio drew on his childhood memories. In such pictures, and in the more daring "Swimmers" (Figure 19) and "Crucifixion" (Figure 20) one cannot fail to be struck by an affinity to the paintings of such Middle European Expressionists of the 1900-1914 period as Heckel, Nolde, Kandinsky and Klee. To imitate such masters (as many have) requires ingenuity, but only genius could achieve similar successes in utter isolation. For like the early Expressionists, José Antônio uses color not to imitate nature but to convey emotion; and his drawing, like theirs, bypasses classic or academic norms to communicate the quintessence of an experience with the fewest possible strokes.

Before going to visit him in his remote home at São Josê do Rio Prêto, I had seen some of these pictures and heard a little about José Antônio's life-style. I had heard that as a young man he whitewashed cemeteries, tamed donkeys, cleaned wells. I had heard that when roses died in his garden he replaced them with plastic buds. I had heard that he played the guitar and watched

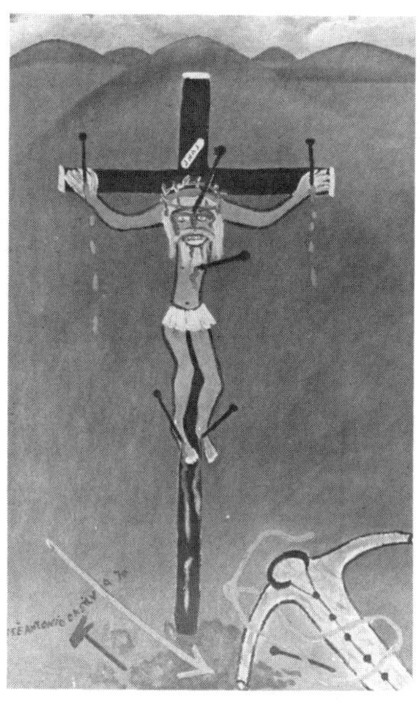

Figure 20. Crucifixion. By José Antônio da Silva. Collection: Crisaldo Morais, São Paulo. Photo: Manu Sassoonian.

soap operas on TV. I had read his shrewd commentary on Christianity: "Christ is the greatest, but nobody wants to be Christ." I had enjoyed as much of his autobiography as I could read, and all of the illustrations. I had heard a little about his private life in the small town ninety miles north of São Paulo with his wife Rosina and their six children, and about his less private life in São Paulo's Hotel Santa Terezinha with the fabled "Maria Clara" of his second novel. And I heard about the war that broke out when Rosina determined to emulate her husband as a famous "primitive" and sold her first picture. (When friends advised the artist that this wifely competition might hurt his prestige and his prices, he had destroyed not only her pictures but her brushes and canvases; whereupon Rosina, in a rage, had annihilated a series of murals in their home in which her husband had depicted their life together.)

I had also seen a recent picture of his with the disc of a long-playing but slow-selling record he had cut peeping from a slot slashed in the canvas—"so that whoever buys the picture will be forced to buy the record too." (As so often with artists of genius, what would be "bad taste" in an ordinary talent, "works": the protruding crescent moon of black acetate in this case gives the tree-trunk an added dimension.) And I had read in a recent letter a description of the apartment he intends to buy in the metropolis, with a barbecue pit for the throwing of parties and a huge library with all the pornographic magazines. "I'll pay in *cruzeiros* for the wildest ones," he had added, "but meanwhile I'm like a dry leaf in the wind, or a garden full of beautiful flowers. I live among great joys and greatsorroleo Without paint I can't create. But without Maria Clara I can't live."

Expectations aroused by such rhetoric, and the slapstick humor of some of the paintings, hardly prepare one for the artist's appearance—or the décor of his home. Portly but not fat, smartly dressed, his thick hair painted black and brushed pompadour style, he was wearing black horn-rim glasses and talking long distance with a client when we came in. Cradling the mouthpiece in his shoulder like any harassed executive (Figure

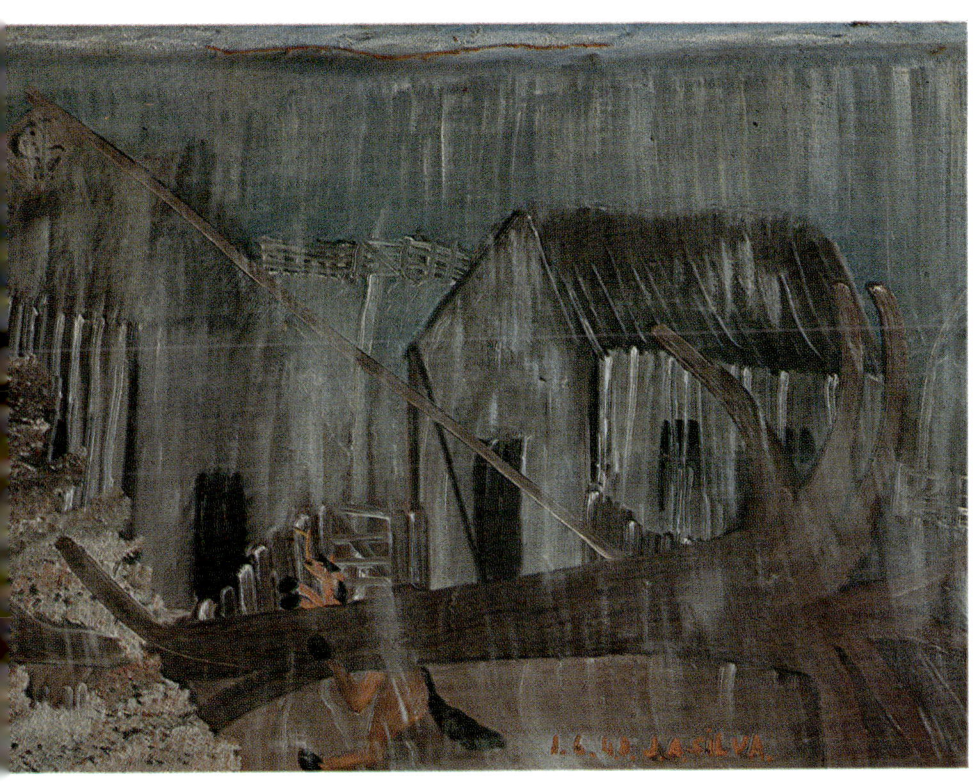

A. Houses in the Rain. By José Antônio da Silva. Museu de Arts Contemporaneo, São Paulo. Photo: Manu Sassoonian.

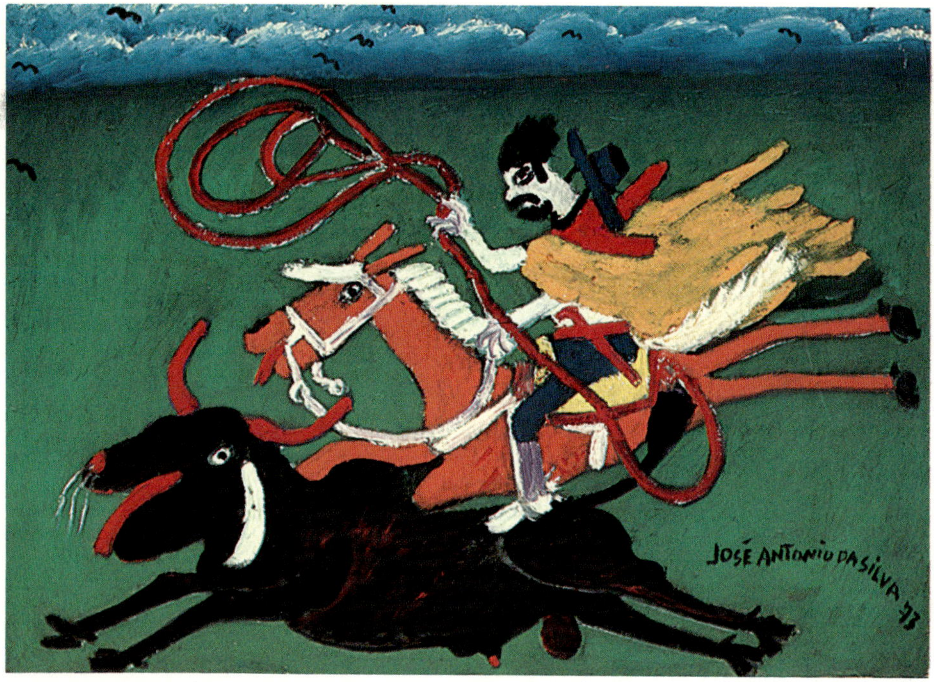

B. 1. Roping the Bull. By José Antônio da Silva. Collection: Artist. Photo: William Negron.

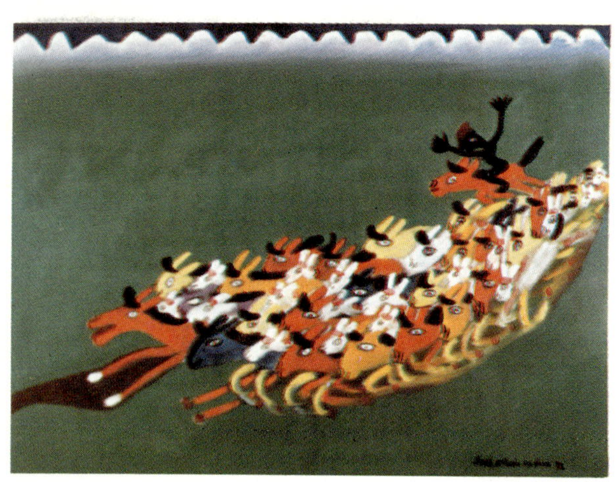

B. 2. Demon Stampeding the Herd. By José Antônio da Silva. Collection: Iraçema Arditi, São Paulo. Photo: Manu Sassoonian.

C. Station of the Cross. By José Antônio da Silva. Church of Nossa Senhora do Sogrado Coração, São José do Rio Prêto. Photo: William Negron.

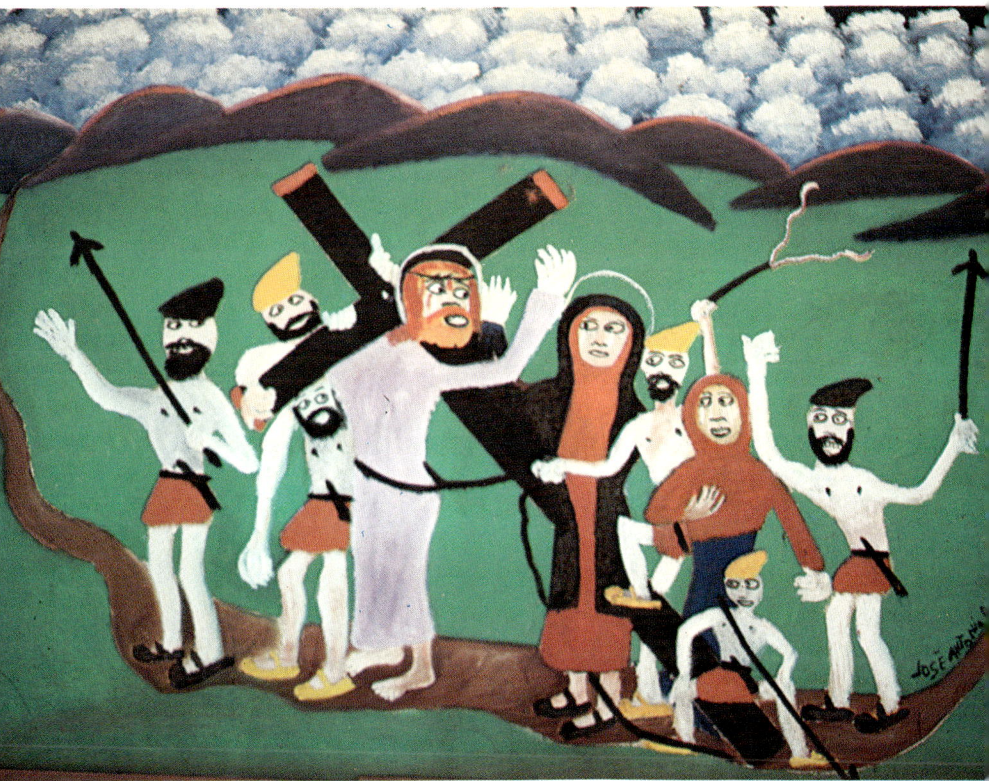

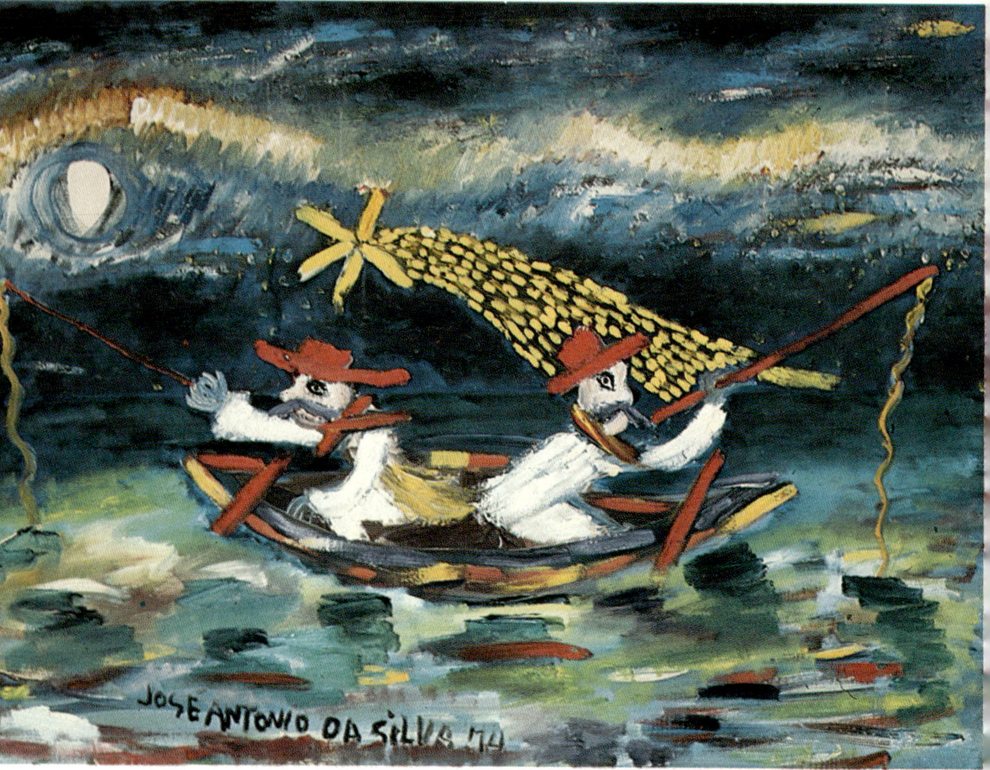

D. Fishing Under the Comet. By José Antônio da Silva. Collection: Artist. Photo: William Negron.

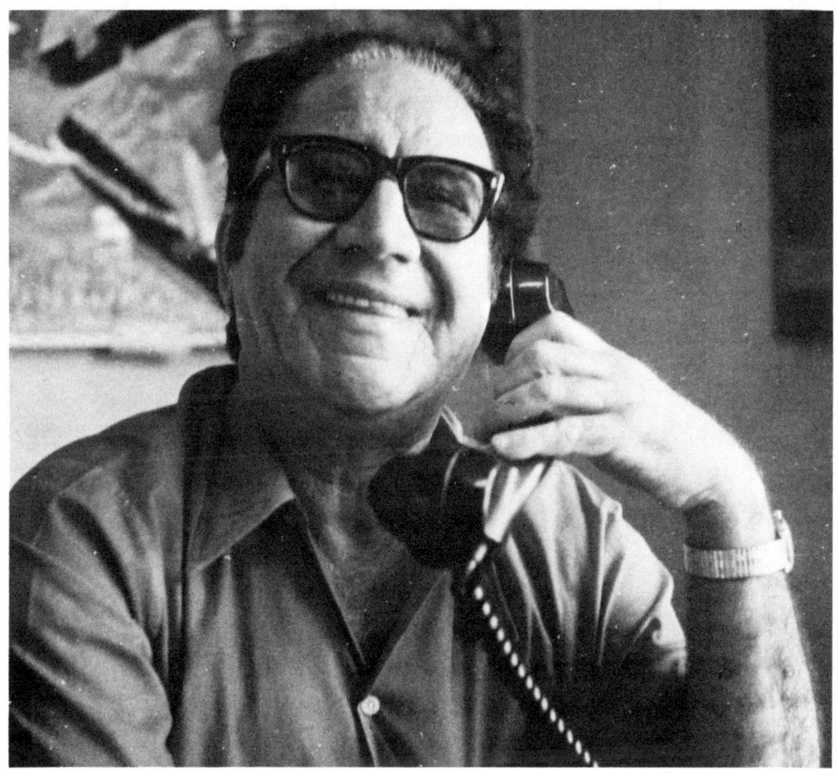

Figure 21. The Artist on the Telephone, São José do Rio Prêto. Photo: Author.

21), he assured us that he'd be right with us and to make ourselves at home.

What José Antônio says and how he says it soon dispels this veneer of propriety. Why was he wearing what appeared to be a surgeon's mask in the row of self-portraits that caught my eye? "The critics try to gag me, but I have ways of getting even, as you'll see! And besides I've learned to make use of my gag." He stepped into a small adjoining room where he paints and came out with a rag covering his face below the eyes. "It keeps out the paint pollution—but not *their* pollution." I looked at the tatters of captioned ribands that swirled about one of these pictures (Figure 22), an expressionist explosion Karel Appel never surpassed in which José Antônio sees himself with a Rip Van Winkle beard and wildly popping eyes: "Watch your neuroses!" "I don't drink or smoke but I adore *morenos*" "Fantasies—the defenses of those being threatened" "The capital is full of bullshit" "This poor creature is being *shot!*" "But he'll shoot back!" etc.

We walked out in the sun-drenched patio and I showed him a photograph of one of his paintings depicting a Kardecist séance. I asked him if he believed in the transmigration of souls.

"My gods are the wind and the sun, and the rain falling before the sun returns. Everbody has these forces inside him, but few know how to release them—with control. I learned everything by myself, nothing in the thirty days I spent in school. Like all unthinking men, I believed in the Christian gods. But that was in Sallis Oliveira where I was born. Here they taught me science, and the rest I picked up eagerly here and there, until finally the Bienal spoiled me and I forgot everything I'd learned. It was only when I saw that they really despised the primitives and were patronizing us for their amusement that I began to learn again what I'd forgotten: that primitive art is pure, like our flag, the color of the Brazilian woods; that the primitive artist's art comes from his heart."

I asked him to play us something on the harmonica or flute. He picked up a guitar and improvised a rhymed song about our visit here to see him. "I taught myself that too, and the violin as well, learning how to compose music and write poems as I went along. You see I grew up among Bahians and Pernambucans. Northeasterners are natural artists so I learned to create as I sang. An artist must be a poet first—whether he paints pictures or composes music—but I don't need to tell you that. The modern art the critics rave about has lost the poetry. Nothing is left in their pictures but the bare bones—fleshless."

"Tell me about your books, José Antônio."

"First I wrote *The Romance of My Life,*" he said. "Then the

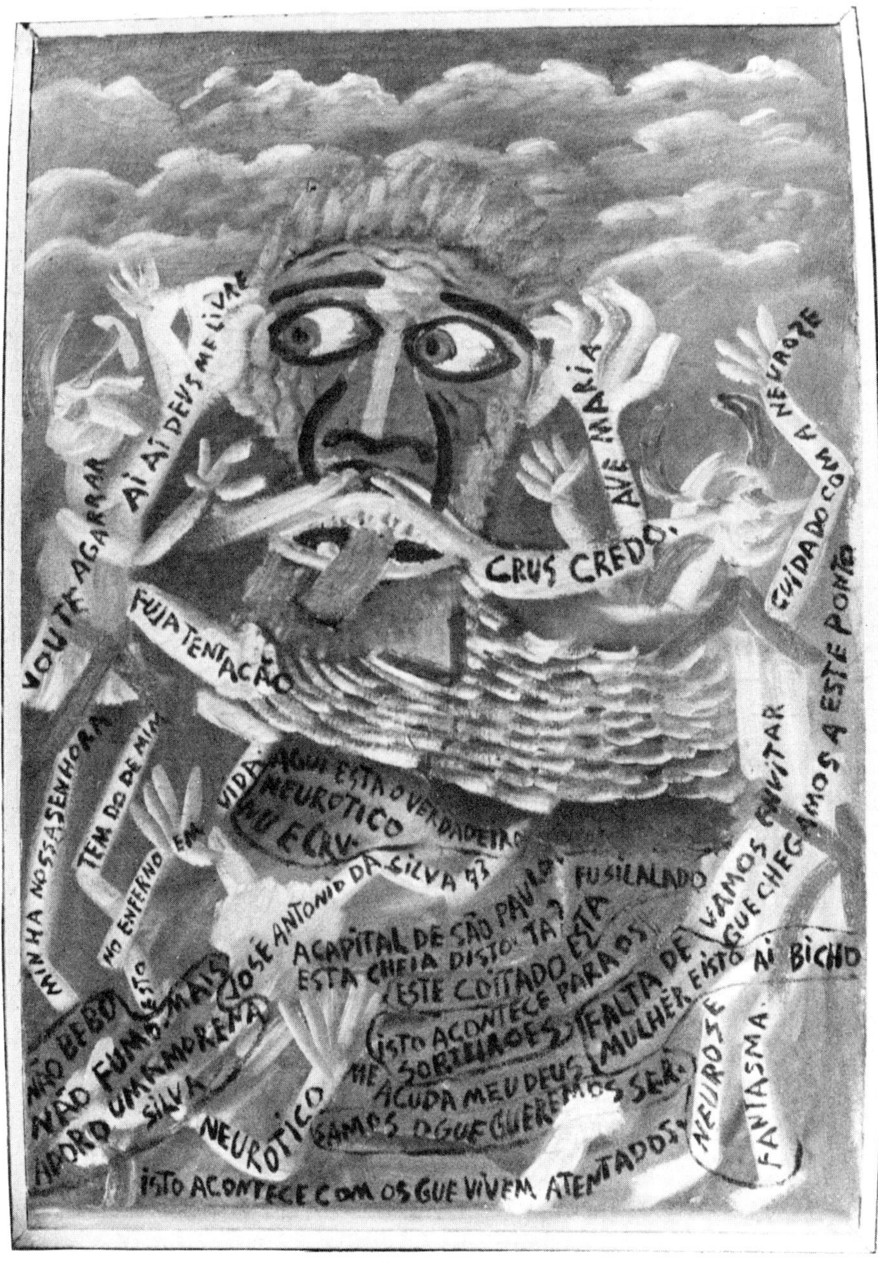

Figure 22. Self-Portrait. By José Antônio da Silva. Collection: Artist. Photo: Author.

novel *Alice,* then the one with pictures in color you like, *Maria Clara*."

I asked him how he could risk using his love's name in view of his wife's notorious jealousy. He smiled.

"That's not her real name. The real 'Maria Clara' boards the bus by pre-arrangement when I go to São Paulo. She never comes here. I don't need *that* kind of warfare!"

"And this new book I hear you're writing?"

"Ah, it's about a lovely girl named Rosanha, shaped like a guitar—"

"Your wife's name, almost."

"Coincidentally. This Rosanha becomes a whore in Panama after a doctor screws her, and then returns to São Paulo with the doctor and his wife—a happy ending!"

"The doctor's wife was happy?"

"Very happy. You see Rosanha paid for his medical degree in Panama with her whoring."

"And then—?"

"Then Rosanha was injured because the doctor's—how you say? penis? was too big, and he suggested an operation to make it smaller, but she wouldn't hear of that. So they all live together happily in São Paulo, and she is still his mistress. I memorized her story in my hotel, the Santa Terezinha in São Paulo, and wrote it here later. When I have the money to print it like the other three books I'll send you a copy."

José Antônio may be momentarily short of funds, but he cut no corners in building this house which outshines all others in this town of 30,000. He made a point of telling us, in fact, that he had spent $70,000 on its construction and furnishings.

The first thing I noticed was that it was divided in two as though each part was separate from the other by one of those invisible protective devices which "Maxwell Smart" used to lower and then forgetfully bang into. The part where we had been talking was José Antônio's "office" lined from floor to ceiling with his pictures for sale, and this wing contained also his cell-like studio, a bathroom, and a large closet stacked with boxes of his books and records, and more pictures. The other, and much larger part of the house, contains the spacious kitchen with frigidaires and freezers. Next to it, off the patio with potted plants, is a formal parlor filled with expensive furniture in a style that might be called Brazilian Grand Rapids, two very large television sets, and a basin with gleaming white porcelain and nickel fixtures set in a niche that gives it the appearance of a kind of shrine. Next to the parlor is a suite of bedrooms with beds lined up as in a dormitory, and a small room with built-in chests and a couch facing a truly mammoth television set where the artist takes his siesta or relaxes watching his soap operas—in Brazil melodramas of infidelity and revenge so overacted that the protagonists seem to be pertpetually making faces at one another as they scream, hurl crockery, or swoon in despair.

Except for a tasteful still life by Rosina, who has started to paint again timidly after last year's holocaust, I saw not a picture in this part of the house. "Why?" I asked the artist.

"They hate my work, the family. Like most unlearned people—"

"But they're happy to live off it—"

"Very happy."

Gliding over the waxed parquet floors, he opened the doors of the bathrooms, gesturing toward the sparkling bidets, glass-doored showers, wall-to-wall mirrors, and then led me into his retreat. "You want to see my clothes?"

I did indeed. He slid back the panels and pulled out the drawers. On one set of hangers were a dozen suits, made to order, and on another several dozen gaudy sport shirts. He took a pair of shoes from a drawerful, handing me one. "Feel the softness of the leather!" Turning to the dressing table on which bottles were arrayed, he pointed to one and then touched his armpits. "My deodorants. An artist must smell good, too."

That afternoon, José Antônio took us to the church of Nossa Senhora do Sogrado Coração to see his Stations of the Cross and meet Padre Francisco Janssen who had commissioned them. I had expected to see murals and was amazed to see the eighteen pictures each only 36-inches wide by 20 high, and hung so far up in the twenty-foot-high archways between the windows of the nave that they could be "read" only with the greatest difficulty. Nor was it possible to photograph them except from a giant stepladder, for each had been bolted to an ugly wall lamp twelve feet off the floor.

In spite of being lost in scale, the paintings are in José Antônio's best style, which is to say magnificent. Probably not since the late Middle Ages or the early Renaissance have these scenes of cruelty, suffering and martyrdom been treated so freshly (Color Plate 2C). The secret of their success is the secret of popular art. The scenes are conveyed not as they might have been, not to glorify a god, and certainly not to glorify an artist by calling attention to his style or scholarship, *but as reality*. In this case, the leader of a peasant rebellion or proscribed cult being given the business by the police along a trail in the backlands as crowds of idlers from town keep pace to watch the fun. The panel showing Christ's family escorting his flower-decked bier from the three croses on the far horizon to an empty grave along a winding path is such a scene as the boy José Antônio must have seen dozens of times on the dusty lanes between Sallas Oliveira and São José do Rio Prêto.

The *vigario* (parish priest) who had commissioned the set and paid the thousands of dollars required without undercutting the artist's São Paulo gallery price of $750 per picture, came out to greet us. I complimented him for his courage for he must surely have flouted the taste of São José's bourgeoisie and outraged their conventional piety.

"I'm sure they like these huge abstract panels you have in the apse much better, eh Padre?"

"Much better!" and then, sensing the irony in my tone of voice, he added: "And you?"

"I think your apse murals would be inoffensive in a third-class provincial restaurant."

He laughed. "They were not my commissioning. I agree."

"Why don't you have José Antônio do the apse, then? On a

grand scale, real murals, after getting rid of these bland atrocities?"

He sighed. "That would not be easy. They're still howling indignantly over this little *Via Sacra*. And the money is used up."

I noticed a sign, in English, on the good priest's desk:

LORD HELP ME TO KEEP MY BIG MOUTH SHUT TILL I KNOW WHAT I'M TALKING ABOUT

But the more convinced Padre Janssen becomes of the rightness of his intuitions, the more his mouth is going to stay open; and get him in trouble. Unless, and until, the great painter's art becomes so widely accepted that some rich donor will pay not only for a glorious apse but for the enlargement of those tiny masterpieces along both aisles.

The canny José Antônio took no chance in running afoul of the *mauvais gout* of the gentry in setting up the town's first Museum of Art. He bought or rented the building, stocked it with his own pictures (and a scattering of others that friends among the populars and sophisticated had given him in exchange for his own). As sole owner, curator, art critic, promoter and guardian, he comes every day with his bunch of keys to open up, collect admissions, and give visiting celebrities the guided tour.

Here hang such of his topical pictures as "Gandhi's Assassin" (the artist clearly identifies with the saint of civil disobedience), "Open Heart Surgery," and the picture already illustrated and described in which the artist's critics at the Sixth Bienal get their just desserts. Over the dangling miscreants in this painting, lest the moral be unclear, a sign reads: DIVINE JUSTICE NEVER FAILS. In the collage (upper left) the artist pointed out to me his admission card to the 1961 show, and two earlier reviews by José Geraldo Viera of *Folha de São Paulo* hailing José Antônio as a master.

"He was the one who threw me out of the exhibit when he saw my latest pictures," the painter muttered with a grim smile. "And here is what will happen to them *after* their bodies are cut down." He pointed to the group of devils in the lower right corner throwing fuel on a fire under an iron cooking pot.

In addition to the painting, the Museum contains glass display cases wth an assortment of oddments: old sewing machines, meat grinders, percolators, slave ankle-cuffs, flat-irons, snake skins, oxen skulls, old license plates. There is also a life-size Crucifixion in concrete by the artist, with barbed wire for the crown of thorns, rusty nails in the palms of the hands, and a kitchen knife plunged to the hilt in the belly with red paint splashed around the wound. José Antônio's iconography is about as subtle as the Bayeux Tapestry, *Strubelpieter,* or a Pluto one-reeler.

Near the door a very large white sandwich-board displays José Antônio's thirty maxims neatly lettered in black under the title PHILOSOPHY OF LIFE. Among them:

> Down with Etiquette!
> Don't trust even yourself.
> Whoever meddles with pigs, eats swill.
> If you want something done, do it yourself.
> The devil is not as ugly as we paint him.
> Nature created the artist.
> The artist created Nature.
> Woman, like the flower, has blossoms and thorns.
> Those who can, go; those who can't, send somebody.
> Man's best friend is his dog.
> Whoever gets there first, drinks clean water.
> The artist never dies; he survives in his art.

José Antônio took advantage of our vehicle to avoid the bus and ride back with us to São Paulo. After playing something for us on the harmonica and tap-dancing to his composition, he packed two enormous valises and put on his best Panama. While he was thus engaged, Bill Negron photographed two unpolemical pictures that I wanted to add to the others just because they joined the best through sheer style. The first of these painterly pictures, "Fishing under the Comet" (Color Plate 2D), recalls the whole gamut of expressive coloration from Van Gogh to De Kooning. The second, a study of trees against a

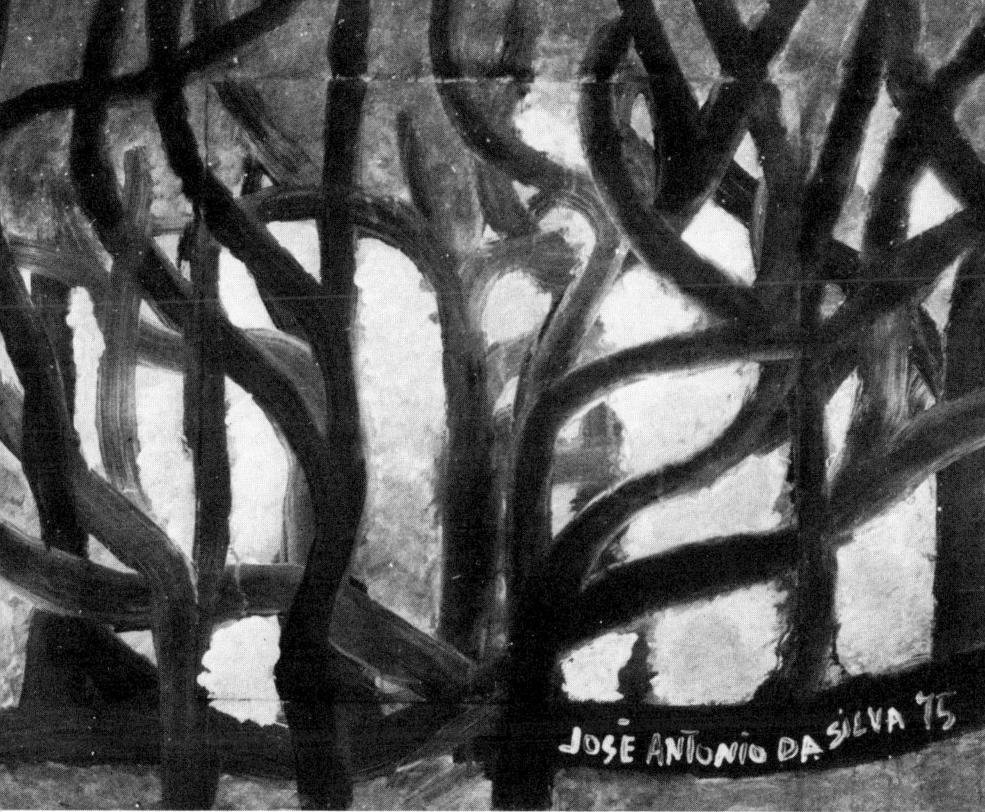

Figure 23. Trees. By José Antônio da Silva. Collection: Artist. Photo: Author.

sunset was spare and nonfigurative but almost as emotional in its impact (Figure 23).

As we settled down in the car for the long ride, I asked José Antônio what he thought of the other popular artists. He hadn't heard of any of the sculptors. And as for the painters, he didn't think any of them measured up to the late Heitor Dos Prazeres. (If José Antônio's empathy for the Rio samba-composer wasn't entirely occupational, he must have recognized a kindred outlook in Dos Prazeres' wacky sense of humor)

"But among the living?" I persisted.

"I go to the Praça Republica now and then, to talk with some of them who are my friends, but the only two in that Sunday fair who seem to have styles of their own are Neuton and Waldomiro (see pp 131, 84)."

"And the big names of Brazilian art," I said, "those who have won some fame abroad—Portinari, for instance..."

"Only two or three of his pictures. The rest are poor imitations of Picasso." (A judgement unkind and overly sweeping, but not without a degree of truth. José Antônio acquired it, no doubt, from some intellectual familiar with the work of both artists, and was parrotting it to me because it neatly disposed of an establishment idol.)

We stopped at a restaurant where the artist wanted to show me some toucans in cages, and he ordered an egg sandwich. He had been telling me about his bad heart condition. I warned him that the cholesterol in the egg might shorten his life. "Eggs help me create," he said, and ordered another. I asked him if he'd been abroad.

"Never."

"And around Brazil?"

"Only to Rio, and to Brasília once by bus. I'm afraid to fly. And besides," rubbing his thumb and forefinger together, "I haven't the money."

"But you're happy with what you have?"

"You wouldn't believe it," he confided as we continued our ride, "but I've contemplated suicide several times. I'd like to get out of São José for good, and settle down somewhere, maybe on the Atlantic at Santos or Guarujá, with Maria Clara."

"Not on a *fazenda*?" I said, as we sped past some luxurious orange- and coffee-plantations.

"No. I'm a country boy who grew up on a farm, so now I need to get away from it, except in my pictures, and live in the city. As long as my mother—"

"I meant to ask you about those pictures of your mother. The two crosses in one—?"

"She was twice widowed."

"And the very elaborate caption in another—?"

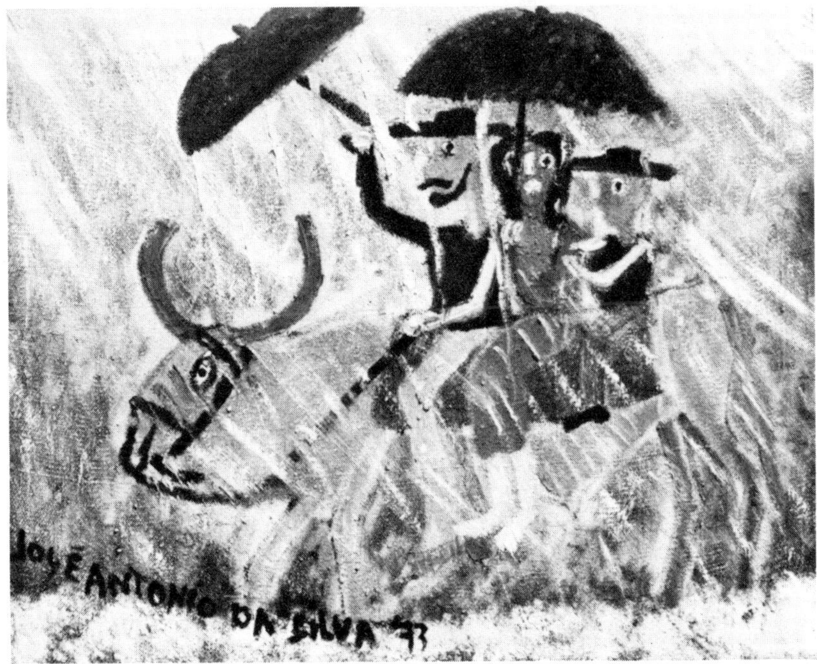

Figure 24. Sunday Morning. By José Antônio da Silva. Collection: Author. Photo: Marilyn Bridges.

"It says: 'My mother is a flower. She made me with love. I miss you mother; you don't know how much.' "

I saw José Antônio for the last time when he paid a courtesy call on me at my hotel. I ordered drinks, and when the waiter brought them, the artist turned to him and pointed to two pictures on my bureau, one a brilliantly decorative head of a *Mãe de Santo* by Terciliano Domingos (see p. 126), the other a little one of his own, showing his family riding an ox in the rain, with his father holding a second umbrella to give their mount better visibility (Figure 24).

"Which is the best?" he asked the waiter.

I was already anticipating what José Antônio would say if the waiter guessed wrong, when the latter, shifting uneasily from one foot to the other as he studied the two paintings, finally indicated José Antônio's.

"You see?" said the artist triumphantly, "everybody can tell!"

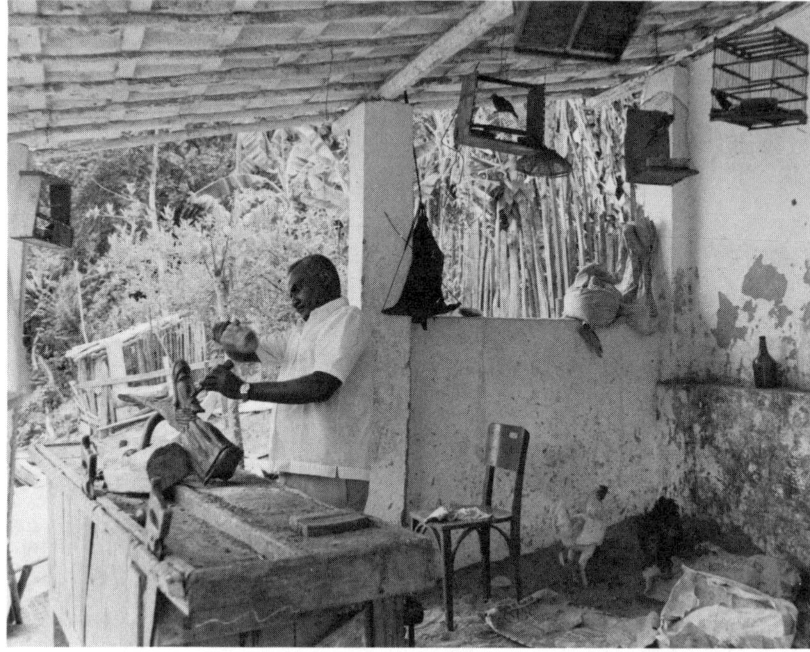

Figure 25. Louco in his workshop, Cachoeira, Bahia. Photo: Manu Sassoonian.

LOUCO

I had heard in Salvador, the Bahian capital, that Louco received his sculptor's name because he spent part of every year in a madhouse. I didn't believe it, but I thought Louco might be amused to hear the question. He laughed. "I was a barber until about ten years ago," he said. "When I stopped shaving heads and started shaving blocks of wood, my neighbors said 'The man is *louco* (crazy).' I couldn't think of a better name for an artist, so I stopped being Boaventura da Silva Filho from that moment."

That was in Cachoeira (Figure 25), a once-prosperous river

port on the Paraguaçu some seventy miles west of Salvador where in Colonial times the sugarcane cut by slaves was loaded onto barges; and then, as the Empire quietly expired and the slaves were freed, by their descendants. Louco's father was among those descendants, and here the sculptor was born January 26, 1932.

From the time when it was the capital of all Brazil, until right down to the present, Salvador has been the fountainhead of the transplanted African cultures. Then and now, *candomblé*, the purest, most stylized and most "African" of the Brazilian cult religions, flourished in this most exotic of Brazilian cities as nowhere else. Louco, whether or not he was ever a true believer, was nourished by the folklore surrounding *candomblé*, attended its gorgeous rites (Figure 26), and saw some of the "miracles," physical and psychic, among those followers of the *Mãe de santo* who believed strongly enough to be "entranced."

Vaudou, the cult religion of the Haitian peasant, is a transplant from Dahomey on the African west coast. *Candomblé* similar in almost every respect and even sharing some of the same gods, was brought over by slaves from the Yoruba and Nago tribes to the south of Dahomey. Neither religion encouraged image-making (Figure 27), though all the original African tribes shared in the great enterprise of carving fetishes from wood; in fact the only visual art commonly practised in both transplanted cults is abstract and geometrical: the making of symbolic diagrams—called *vevers* in Haiti, *pontos riscados* in Brazil—to help in invoking a particular deity. How, then, did the cult religion help to inspire popular artists like Louco, when none of its imagery was figurative? and by what route and through what forms was such a mysterious connection effected? Writing of Haitian art, Pierre Apraxine deals with this paradox convincingly:

> For the voodoo worshipper nothing is invisible, nothing is in need of representation. There is no supernatural world because all worlds—the immediate and the beyond—are simultaneously present, natural and accessible to the eye. Writing on Haiti, Edmund

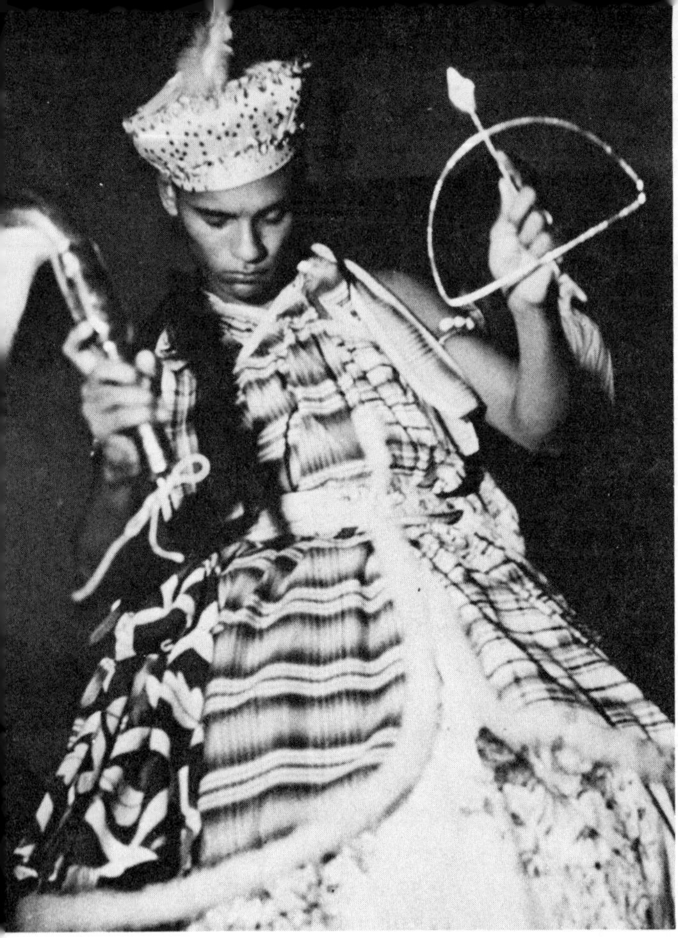

Figure 26. Figures in a *candomblé*, Salvador da Bahia. Photos: Embassy of Brasil, Washington.

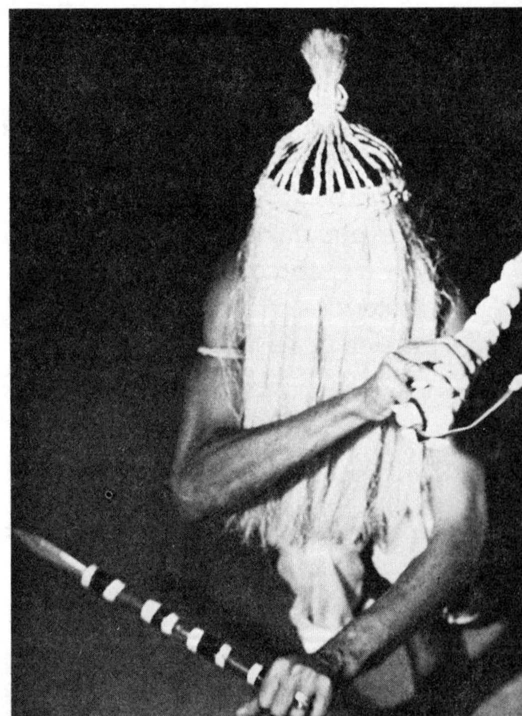

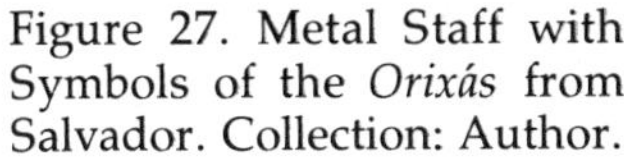

Figure 27. Metal Staff with Symbols of the *Orixás* from Salvador. Collection: Author.

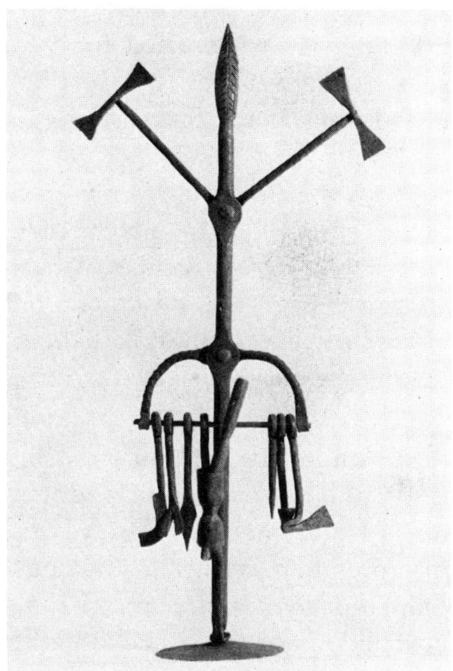

Wilson has observed that for the Haitian "the immediate thing was the supernatural world...and what we call the real world no more than a symbolization of events in the world of religious myth."

How, then, was this culture able to move "from the absence of visual art to the concentrated activity of painting convincing enough to command world attention?" The answer, Apraxine continues,

> ...may lie in the fact that the absence of visual art among the Haitian masses depended, for the most part, on a state of cohesive and undifferentiated consciousness subsumed under the voodoo religion: individual and collective identity were one and the same.

In contrast to the popular masters of other countries who were all isolated one from another and were mainly reacting against the fragmented consciousness of technologized societies with arts long since detached from life, the artists of the Haitian renaissance were making the transition from the invisible state of folkways to the formal visions of individual painters:

> They were moving *away* from the undifferentiated consciousness of the collective life toward the individuality of paintings by which they were identified. What a Douanier Rousseau and Obin share as "naive" painters is their totally individual styles, while siphoning their images from the collective consciousness and their inspiration from the real or imagined life of the people.[1]

Substitute José Antônio da Silva for Rousseau, Djanira for Obin, and Louco for Liautaud, the great *vaudou*-inspired sculptor of Haiti whose work Apraxine does not deal with, and his interpretation applies to Brazil as exactly as to Haiti. As with Liautaud (see Figure 3, p.   ), there is no trace of the symbolic abstractions of the transplanted African cults in the Brazilian artist's sculptures, but a deep, pervasive religious expressionism going far beyond the occasional "representation" of specific *candomblé* spirits. Moreover the "syncretism" with which both transplanted African religions have accommodated their gods to the gods and saints of official Roman Catholicism enables both Liautaud and Louco to make occasional "Crucifixions" and "Virgin Marys" with a convincing power no longer available to these artists working within the exhausted tradition of Western Christian art.

Behind Louco's "Virgin with Penitent Angels" (Figure 28) one senses simultaneously the emotion appropriate to a Mother of Mankind, compassionately grieving for the tribulations of her children, and the *Mãe de Santo* of *candomblé* sheltering her *filhas*

[1]*Haitian Painting: The Naive Tradition*. Catalogue to an exhibition sponsored by the American Federation of Arts, selected and prefaced by Pierre Apraxine, Assistant Curator of Painting and Sculpture, The Museum of Modern Art. New York, 1973. For a description of the imagery of Haitian sculptors, similarly cult-inspired, see *The Miracle of Haitian Art* by the present writer.

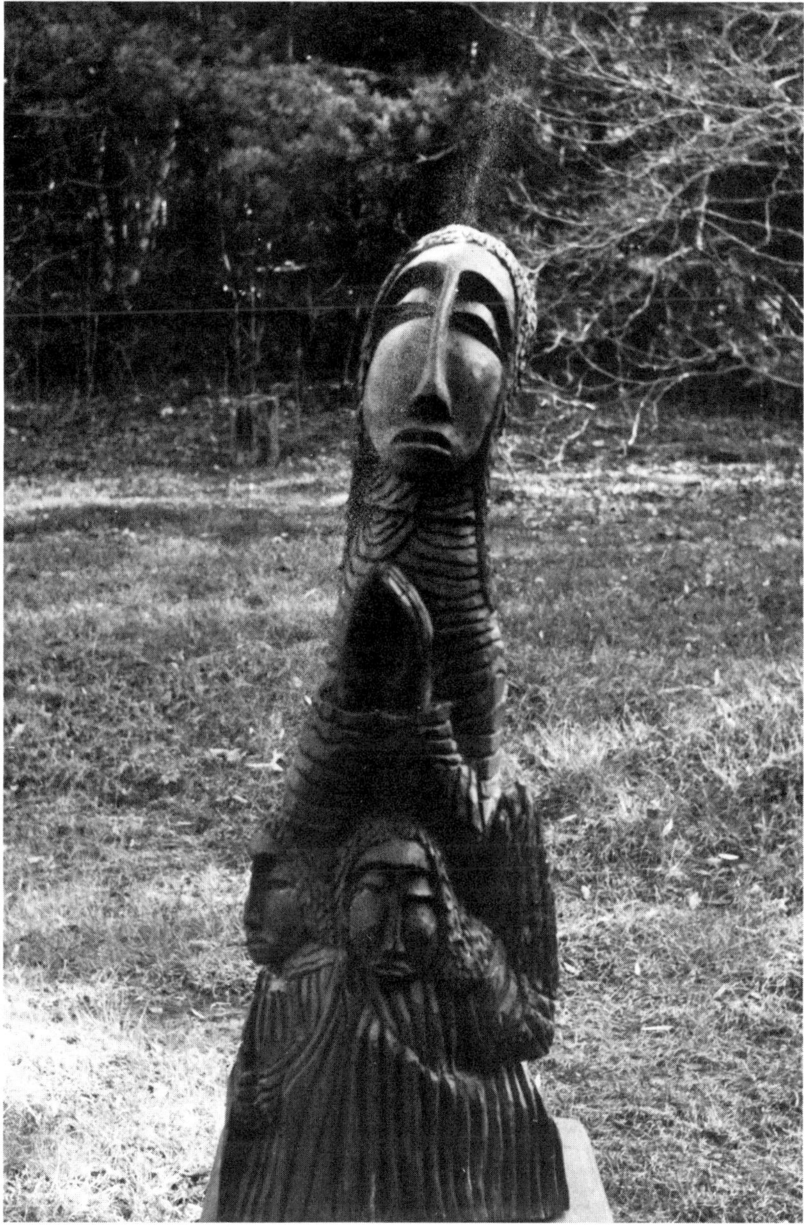

Figure 28. Virgin with Penitent Angels. By Louco. Collection: Author. Photo: William Negron.

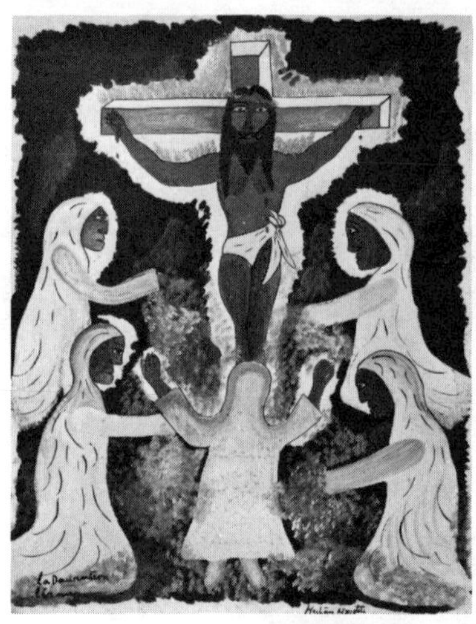

Figure 29. Crucifixion. By Hector Hyppolite. Musée de l'Art Haïtien, Port-au-Prince, Haiti.

Figure 30. Apostle Seamen. By Louco. Collection: Augusto Rodrigues, Rio de Janeiro. Photo: William Negron.

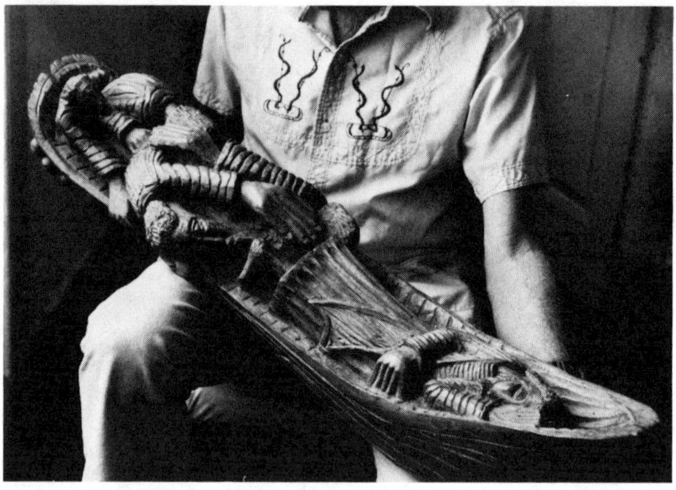

against "possessions" inimical to their welfare and the welfare of all true believers. But it is the elongated features common to the great tradition of African sculpture and surviving in the long-slumbering Bahian racial memory, that gives the piece its monumental poise devoid of sentimentality. Hector Hyppolite, the Haitian priest of *vaudou,* whose art so entranced André Breton, revitalized Christian iconography with the same "African" sensibility (Figure 29).

Similarly, in such an early Louco sculpture as the "Apostle Seamen" from the collection of the painter Augusto Rodriguez in Rio (Figure 30), Louco invests the familiar Christian story of the terrified fishermen on the Sea of Galilee with all the conviction and plastic power of the mediaeval Gothic craftsmen. How? By identifying this experience with experiences familiar to humble fishermen on the ocean and rivers of Bahi, and the overall meaning of their miraculous escape from death with the intercession of the *candomblé* spirits invoked by boatmen in Salvador and Cachoeira.

When Louco, on the other hand, depicts such a cult spirit directly, as in his image of Iemanjá, the goddess of the sea, being raised from her watery habitat by devoted attendants (Figure 31), the sculptor is drawing, unconsciously no doubt, on the spirit of compassion in Christ's teachings that plays no role in the African cult.

Two ingredients of his style that Louco draws from neither

Figure 31. *Iemanjá* Assisted from the Sea. By Louco. Collection: Author. Photo: Marilyn Bridges.

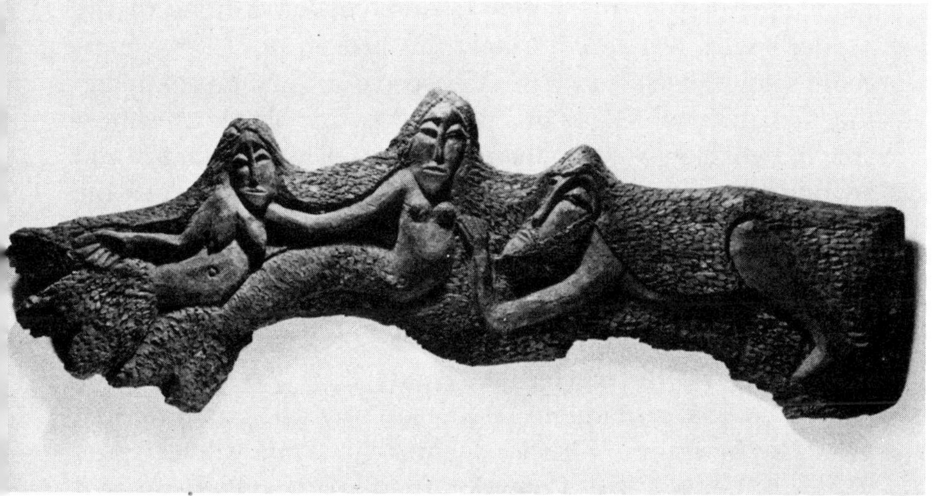

religion, but that are inventions of his genius for sculpture alone, are his use of the concentric rings of the wood (hard jacaranda for the most part) to convey facial expression, grief especially, and his ingenious splintering to give the effect of streaming hair or fragmented waves.

Louco was born in Cachoeira in 1929 but it wasn't until 1965 when he was 36 that he made his first sculpture.

"I began carving pipes out of wood and clay," he told me, "to keep busy when I wasn't barbering. I began to improve the pipes with faces and figures. Then they got so big they were no longer pipes! Roberto—whose last name I can't recall; he was one of the restorers of old houses here—was the first to encourage me. He showed some of those early things to Jorge Amado and Mário Cravo, Jr. and soon they were buying everything I carved. Now I sell my things right here, and so does my brother 'Malouco', and my son and nephews, all of whom have taken up carving."

I had seen some of their work the week before in Salvador's Iron Market, and in the same stall where I had bought my first Louco, a "Head of Christ." Rather appalled by the perfunctory quality of the new carvings, I asked incredulously whether they were indeed Louco's work. The proprietor of the stall, to my relief, finally admitted that they were all by "Malouco" and other members of the family. "And you have none of the Master's work?" I asked. "Only this broken piece," the merchant said, "which I am about to sweep out," and he pointed to the "Iemanjá" which lay in a pile of dust and shavings, almost split in two. He was more than happy to sell it to me for $20 and an hour later in my hotel room I had glued and wired the magnificent relief adequately enough to satisfy the most picky museum curator.

Louco remembered the piece well and was glad to hear that I had given it a second life. I had already bought from him the large "Virgin with Angels" (see Figure 28, p. 79) for which he had asked $55, and Manu Sassoonian, my photographer that year, had brought a "Crucified Christ" in white wood (Figure 32) for somewhat less. I mention these prices only because it

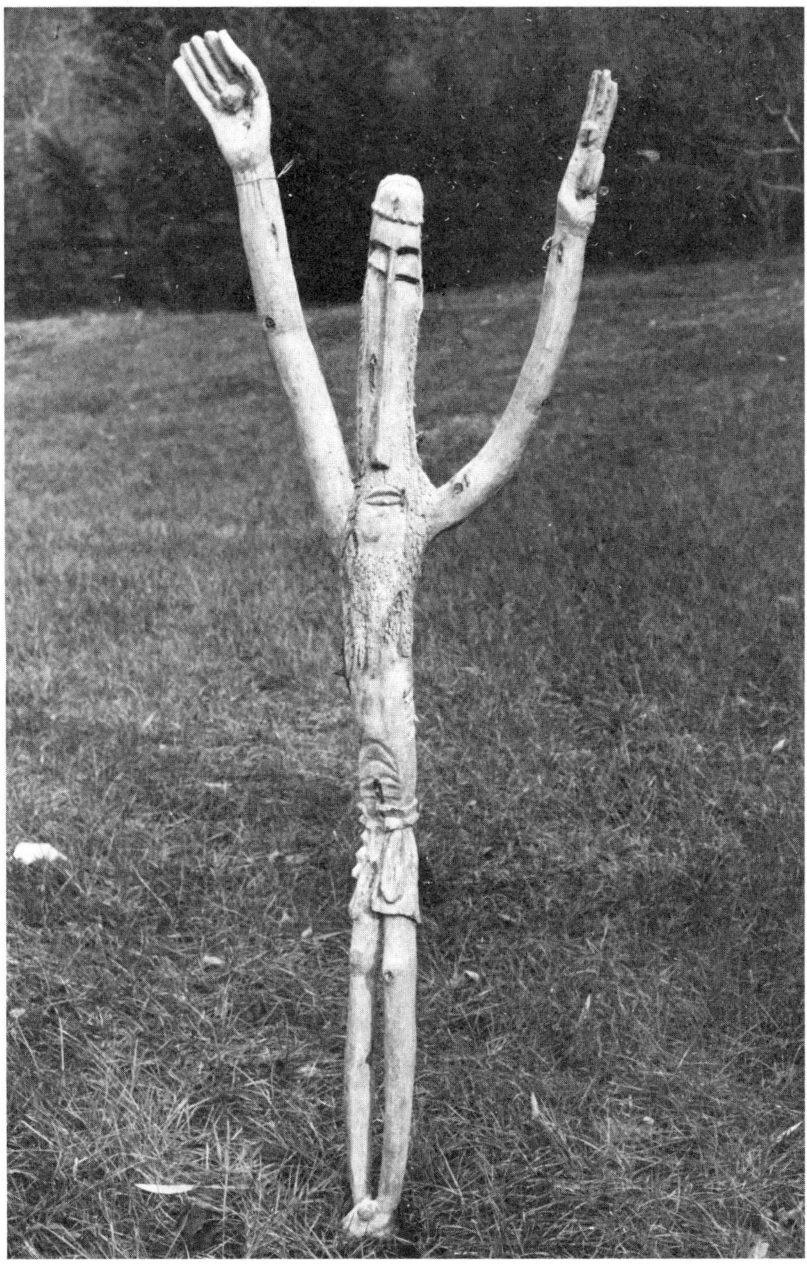

Figure 32. Crucified Christ. By Louco. Collection: Manu Sassoonian. Photo: William Negron.

highlights a problem most popular artists have to face, a problem often crucial to their survival *as artists.* Louco asked me whether I thought he was charging too little, and whether he should deal exclusively with a gallery and perhaps move to Salvador. I told him that he should raise his prices, at least to approximate the prices the galleries in Rio and Recife were charging; and that he would do well to stay away from the big cities where too much of his time would be consumed with merchandizing, and where demands might be made on him to change his style or repeat his successful subjects. "You work so well here," I added, "where your roots are, that you might lose some of your inspiration among the wheelers and dealers."

He agreed, and as we moved out to his airy workshop to photograph him chisel in hand, I asked him where his religious beliefs lay.

"I belong to all religions," he said. "When I was young I attended many *candomblés,* but I attended Mass too, regularly. Now I am too busy expressing my devotion to the holy spirits through my carvings to attend religious ceremonies. I hope God will forgive me."

"You mean—the gods?"

"Yes," he replied with a serene smile, "the gods."

I asked him who the personages were in a blocky sculpture he was working on with two large figures above three smaller ones.

"Above you have Jesus and his Mother. Below are those who betrayed them: a soldier, a policeman, and a lawyer.

In addition to his deeper intuitions, it was clear that the great sculptor had a pretty good understanding of this world's political realities.

WALDOMIRO DE DEUS

When does the popular artist stop being "popular"? Answer: When he elects to join the establishment and pays his admission charges by playing formal or intellectual games. In Brazil as elsewhere, there are so many self-taught artists or failed academicians of the avant-garde engaged in this kind of slight-of-hand that is is not easy to be sure about the border-line cases.

Until I visited him in his home and saw for the first time a large number of his paintings together, I was not sure about Waldomiro de Deus. Was his demonology synthetic? I knew that he had visited Italy. Were these huge, violently contorted figures, with their undifferentiated features, rolling eyeballs, and lascivious gestures put together out of a familiarity with Pisa and Orvieto? Was this the *ersatz* Campo Santo of *candomblé*? Or had Waldomiro entrusted his soul to Signorelli by the same rules of necromancy as Arigó, the entranced surgeon of Congonhas, who yielded his identity to "Dr. Fritz" at those precise moments when he performed his miraculous operations with a rusty knife? Perhaps. But then again, it could be no more than fast brushwork on the part of a painter shrewed enough to anticipate the new direction art was about to take.

These speculations and unkind surmises faded the moment I found Waldomiro at work in the "commune" he had brought with him from the fecund Northeast.

To appreciate the impact—well, imagine if you can, coming upon a colony of Ninth Century Mayas building a temple to the sun in the courtyard of a Chicago tenement—one must have seen São Paulo. São Paulo is the biggest city in the world south of the equator, approaching Tokyo and Los Angeles in population, and with more pollution and traffic tangles than either. Flying into it from Buenos Aires to the south or from Rio de Janeiro to the north, its thousands of skyscrapers climb up and down the foothills as far as the eye can see in every direction. Driving *out* of it, to the port of Santos or the beach resort of Guarujá fifty-nine miles east, the 8-lane superhighway pierces such a concentration of petrochemical plants and blast furnaces that it is sometimes necessary to turn on one's headlamps at high noon just to glimpse the vehicle ahead through the orange smog. São Paulo has more art museums, more art galleries, more good artists, more bad artists, and many more art critics than all the cities of South American combined. It has the best informed and most enlightened newspaper south of *The New York Times*. And it is completing a subway system which is not expected to make a dent in the appalling congestion created by a seemingly endless lemming-like flow of unemployed and unemployables from the pampas of Rio Grande do Sul to the jungles of Amazonas.

Now picture yourself taking a taxi and driving for an hour through a *walpurgisnacht* of fuming, roaring trucks to the outlying district of Osasco, and driving around for another hour trying to locate the street among streets with no name signs, and the house among houses with no numbers. When you find it finally, you knock on a latched gate and are prepared (or unprepared) for your first shock. The gate opens and you see, at the bottom of a winding alley with concrete ramps and shacks on both sides, a peasant woman drawing water in a chained bucket from a *well*.

Bemused by this unlikely apparition, you are guided forward by the comely black girl who opens the gate until your eye catches through an open shutter on the right a wall covered with life-size figures attending some kind of bridal ceremony: figures vividly clothed, the whites of their eyes staring out at you seeming to provide the only illumination (Figure 33).

A low but reassuring laugh from across the passageway makes you turn. Through an iron grill in a red door you see a face (Figure 34). The door opens and Waldomiro steps out to greet you. Shirtless, barefoot, an athletically built young man with an Afro and wearing satin bodypants with bell bottoms, his body is bronzed to coppery red.

He greets us in Italian, and then, seeing our hesitation, shifts to idiomatic French. I express my astonishment at the glimpse of the mural and a wish to see more. Another smile lights up his open features.

"Wait! You've see nothing!"

Taking a bunch of keys from his pocket, and putting one finger to his lips dramatically, he opens the shack below it. The blazing sunlight streams in but barely reveals the corners of the

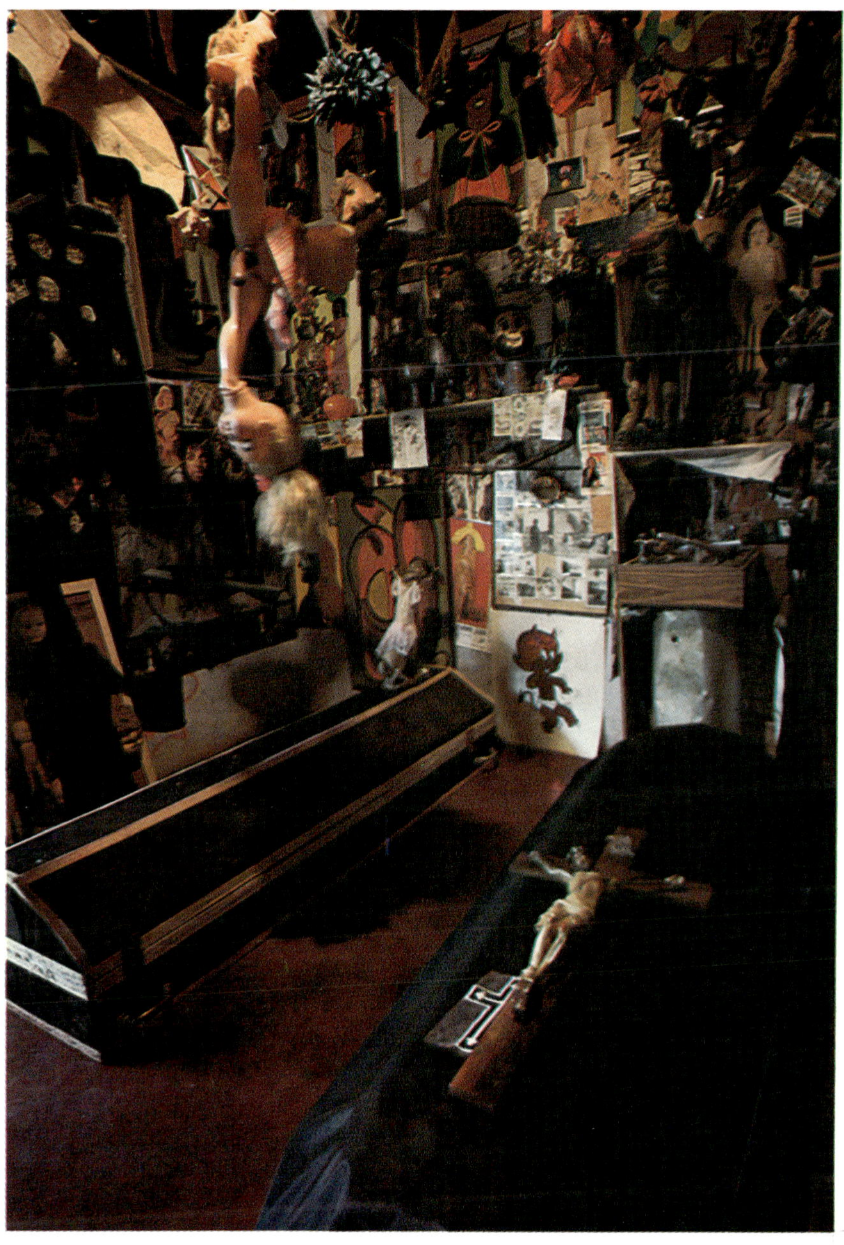

A. Chamber with Caskets and Fetishes. Assemblage by Waldomiro de Deus. Home of the Artist, Osasco, São Paulo. Photo: William Negron.

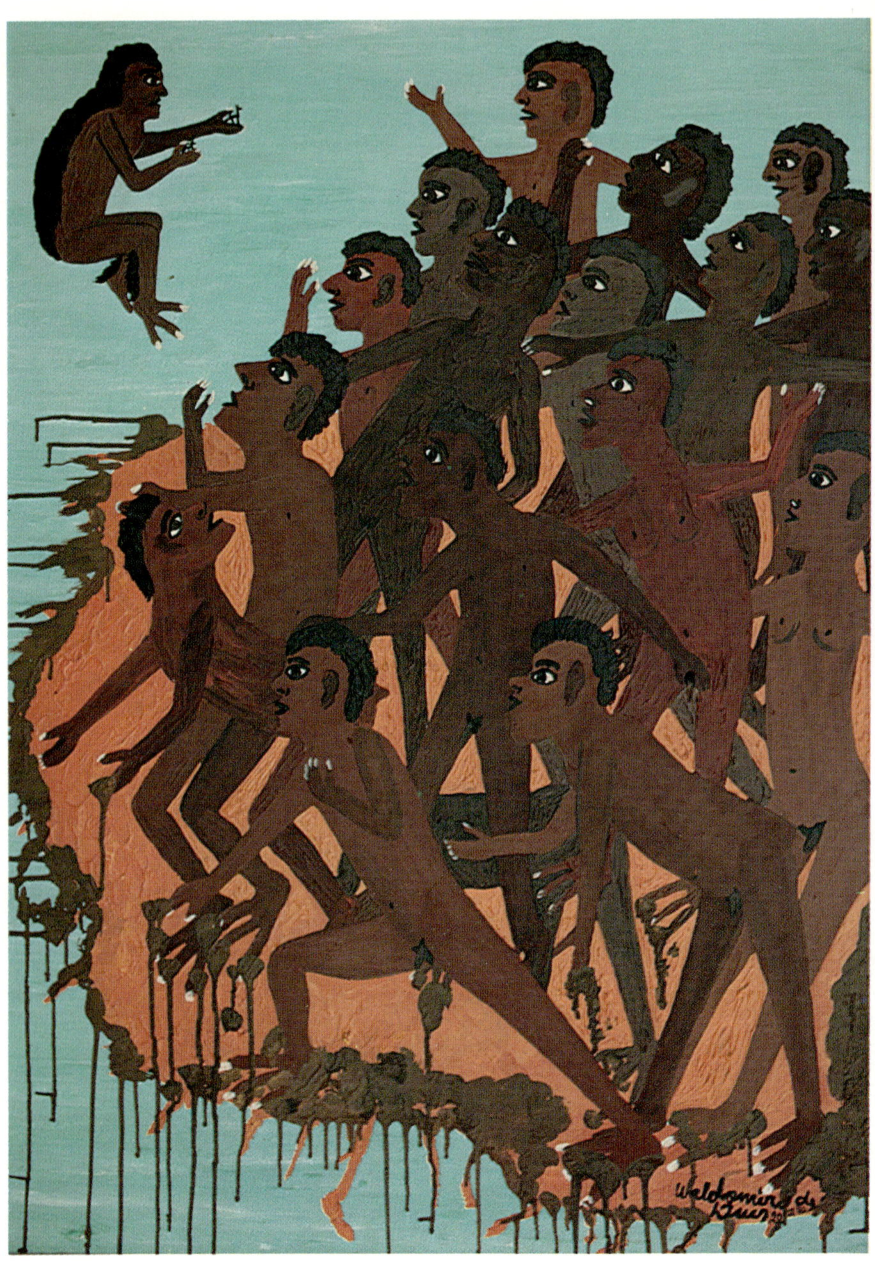

B. When the Devils were Expelled from Heaven and Came to Earth. By Waldomiro de Deus. Collection: Artist. Photo: William Negron.

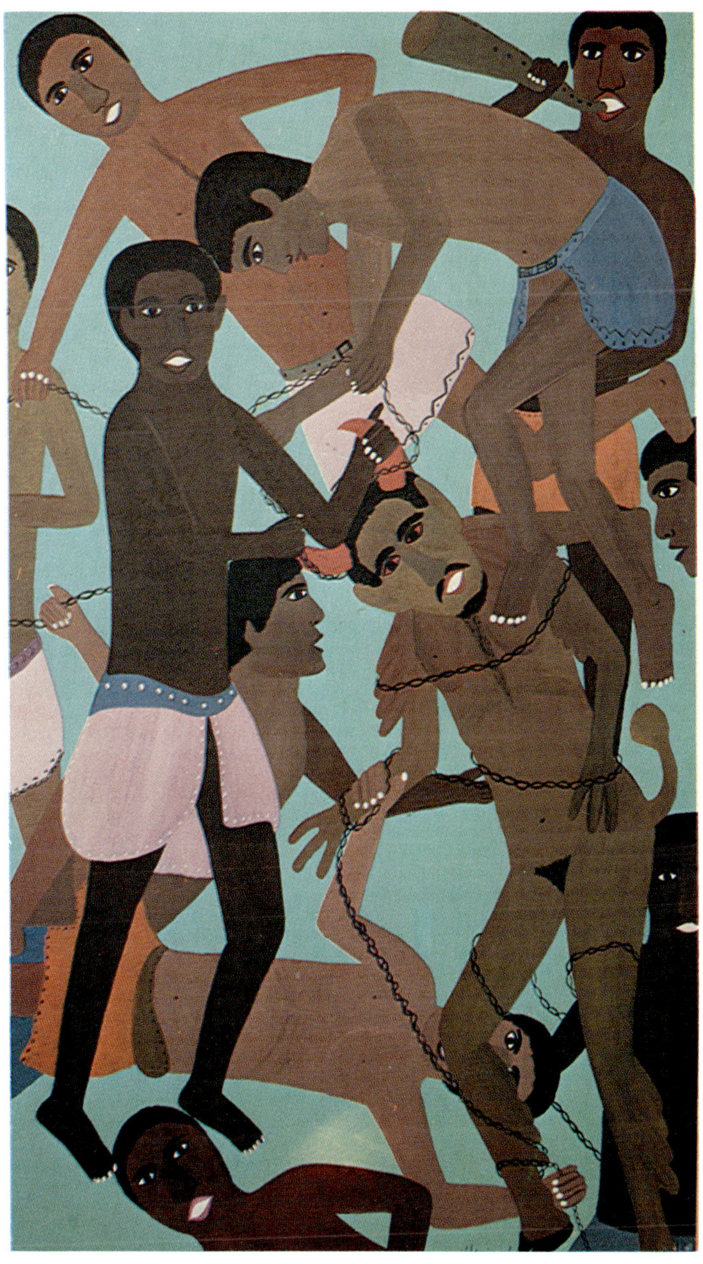

C. Creation of Devils. By Waldomiro de Deus. Collection: Artist. Photo: William Negron.

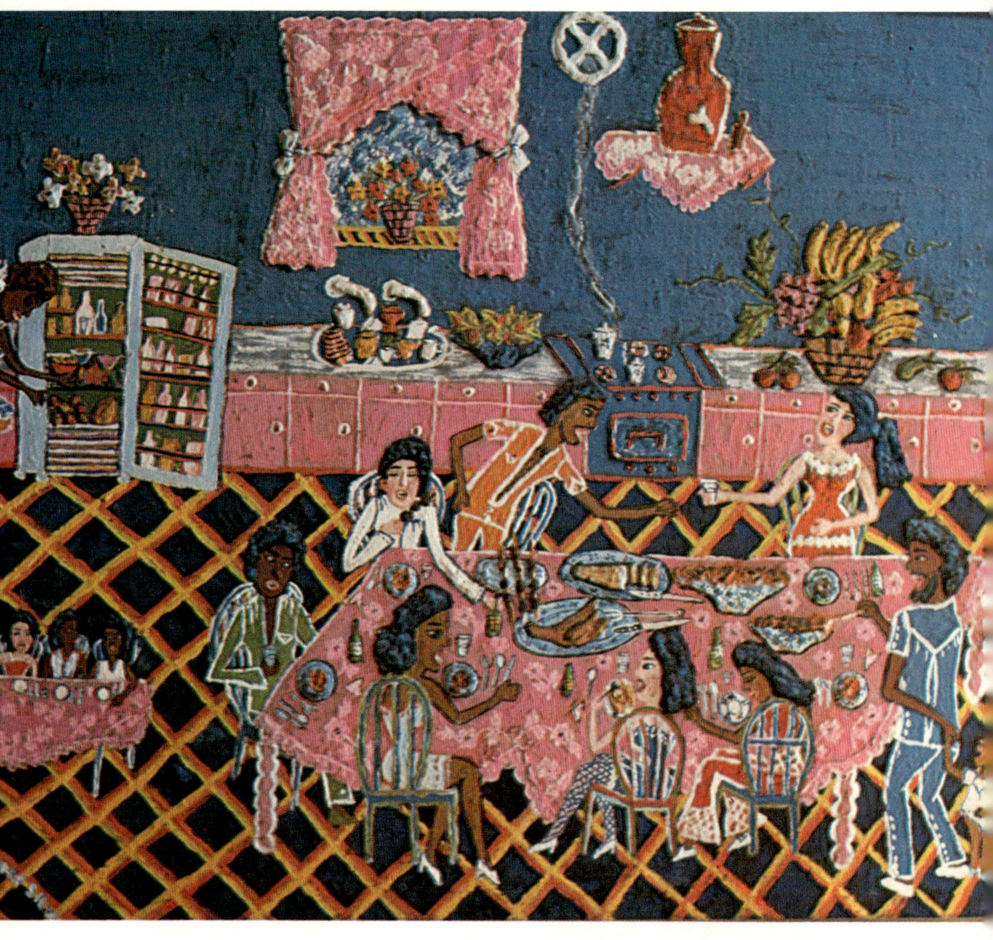

D. Family Dinner. By Maria Auxiliadora Silva. Collection: Renée and Daniel Sasson, São Paulo. Photo: William Negron.

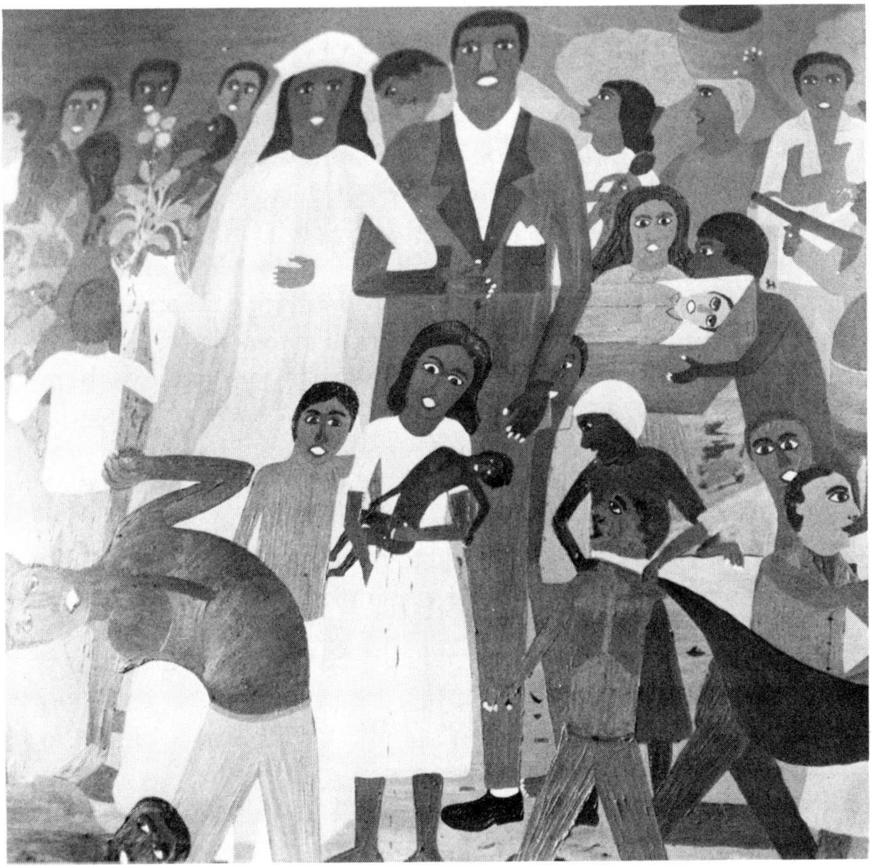

Figure 33. (above) Mural of Bridal Group (detail). By Waldomiro de Deus, Osasco, São Paulo. Photo: Author.

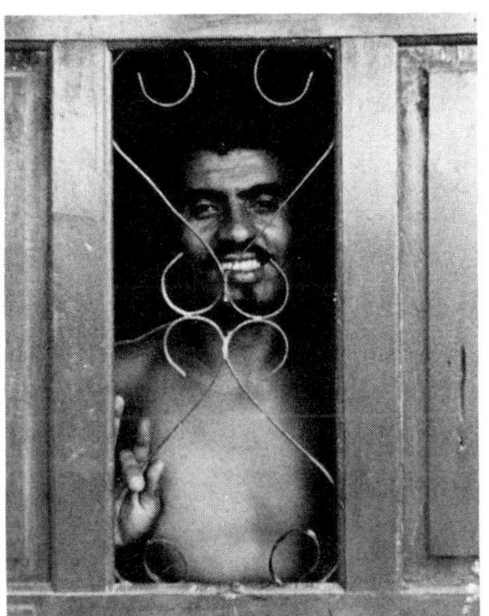

Figure 34. The Artist in the window of his Osasco home. Photo: William Negron.

windowless room whose walls, ceiling and floor are painted black. From the cobwebbed ceiling, and swaying slightly in the breeze, dangle a weird assortment of fetishes: skulls of cows and donkeys, thigh bones with gristly sinews, wooden heads (*ex votos*) from Ceará, moulded tarantulas larger than life and covered with realistic hair, stone carvings of detached hands and feet, and in the center eerily highlighted by the entering wedge of sunlight, a large female china doll half-clothed in white lace and satin, hanging by one foot, blond hair streaming, and with a rubber penis strapped to its *mons veneris*. Painted figures could now faintly be discerned on the walls, and in the center of the black floor stained red in splotches lay two adult-size caskets with nickel handles, the lid of one half open (Color Plate 3A).

Oddly enough the effect upon us of all this necrophilic assemblage was neither sick nor pornographic but religious in an inexplicably moving way. I turned to the artist who was watching our reaction curiously and asked him who the empty coffins were for.

"For us."

"When you die?"

"No. While we live."

"You sleep in one?"

"Not now. The weather is too cold. But when it's warmer."

"And the other one?"

"Whoever wants it. My girl friend. My mother. Even my grandmother who is over a hundred. They all enjoy its use from time to time."

"To accustom themselves to death?"

"Perhaps. But more from the feeling of contentment (*félicité* was the French work he used) it gives one. To be ready. Without fear."

"You're a Christian, Waldomiro?"

"Not exactly. I do believe in God, and in the devils—as you will see from my paintings."

We moved down the ramp to the series of shacks that contained the family's living quarters. Two large salons were hung from floor to ceiling with several dozen garishly colored but firmly composed and drawn canvases, many of them huge. To get them off the walls, through the narrow door and into the sunny courtyard by the well where they could be photographed was an hour's grueling work. The artist wanted to do it all, but of course we wouldn't let him. The titles of the pictures, which I jotted down while Bill Negron set up his tripod and began snapping, indicate Waldomiro's preoccupations:

"When the Devil was Expelled from Heaven and Came to Earth." (Color Plate 3B)

"Christ's Second Coming." (A caption adding: "God gives the key to Christ. When the harp is played, we will cease to exist.")

"Creation of Devils." (Color Plate 3C).

"Death of a Bull."

"Angels Chaining a Devil." Etc., etc.

In an adjoining parlor were paintings by José Antônio da Silva, and other friends among the local popular artists who had exchanged pictures with Waldomiro: Ivonaldo, Maria Auxiliadora Silva, Gerson de Souza. I admired especially an intricate painting of jungle birds and flowers by Isabel de Jesús, and Waldomiro confided that he hoped to marry that artist soon—"if she'll move in here with me."

"You've been married before?"

"Six times."

"Legal marriages?"

"Well, more or less legal!"

"Children?"

"None so far."

We asked him to introduce us to his family, and while his sister was assembling them for a group picture I asked him to explain the small dogs that appeared in many of the pictures.

"They're dogs that died in my house over the years. I don't want to forget them."

"And the pictures that caused such a scandal a few years ago when you started to paint, those seven-foot "Virgin in Mini-Skirts" and "Christ in Dungarees?"

"Those were my declaration of independence, you might say. Now I can settle down to painting the real me."

He introduced his mother and father; then the grandmother, aged 105, and the grandfather, aged 115, both spry and with faces comparatively unwrinkled. Neither of them, Waldomiro told us, had ever been to a doctor. "When sick, they brew leaves from certain plants and trees."

The grandmother at first declined to pose with the others. I asked her why.

"Because I'm too ugly. Why do you want me?"

"Because you're the grandmother of a great artist."

She smiled and took her place in the lineup (Figure 35).

Waldomiro had brought his whole family here, to share in his good fortune, as soon as he began to support himself from the sale of his pictures. They had come the thousands of miles by truck with all their belongings from the tiny village where he was born, Massaranduba, some six hundred miles due west of Salvador in the backlands of Bahia.

Unlike any other popular artist, with the exception of Rousseau, Waldomiro's paintings gain power in proportion to their size. This may be, in Waldomiro's case, because he now focuses on giving shape to his dreams almost exclusively. Dreams are peopled by shadowy figures, often; figures that move through rooms without cracks in the wall, landscapes defined by a single tree. Often their features are indistinguishable, or seem merely disturbingly familiar. What is happening is more important than what is there. Such are the neurotic ghosts that flit through Munch's paintings—who remembers what they look like? Only their expressions are memorable. Or Fuseli's nightmares. Or El Greco's ecstatic visions—his saints are look-alikes. Or the Byzantine Christs, those awesome symbols of majesty. Or Rousseau's "Sleeping Gypsy" (see Figure 1, p. 18), the dream incarnate. Leonardo suppressed *his* famous dream, Freud tells

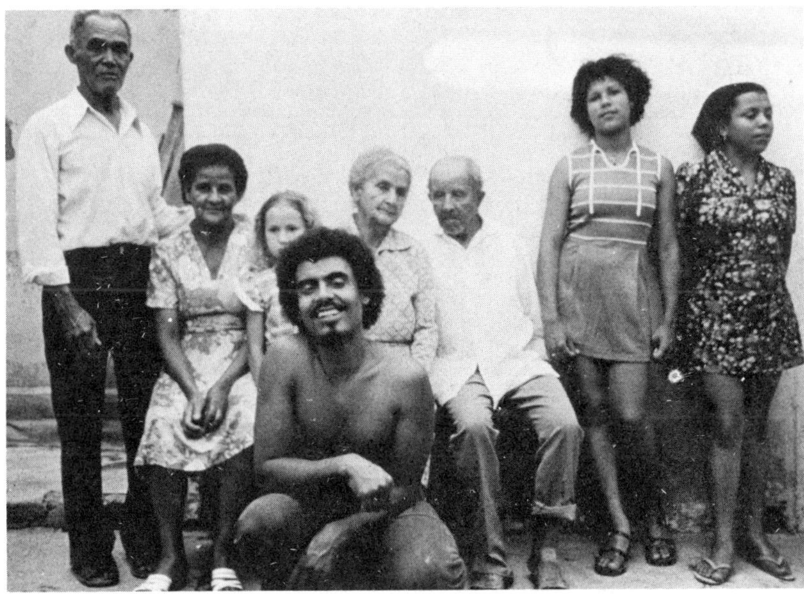

Figure 35. Waldomiro de Deus with his family. Osasco, São Paulo. Photo: William Negron.

us, but the figures with half-smiles that haunt his eerie landscapes are somnambulists without personalities.

So it is with Waldomiro's macabre protagonists. How absurd they would look in José Antônio da Silva's *paulista* countryside, or in one of those boarding-house rooms he paints with an iron bed on which a naked tart sits telephoning her client while a jolly skeleton in the corner rattles his bones! Or walking down the street in one of those busy Flemish villages alive with Breughel's passion for facts. But in the nocturnal world of Waldomiro's troubled visions his *personae* are perfectly appropriate and they "do their thing" with all the sensual sadism and lightfooted rhythm of the sleepwalkers they are.

GTO

The sleepy town of Divinópolis where nothing has ever happened and no sightseer ever goes, is comparable in size to São José do Rio Prêto, and shares with that somnolent hamlet of the next state to the south one distinction: it is the habitat of genius.

As in the case of São José do Rio Prêto, Divinópolis is only a few hours drive on an excellent highway from the state capital—in this case Belo Horizonte, a skyscraper city of over a million from which the state of Minas Gerais is administered—but as far as the citizens of that most modern of Brazilian cities are concerned, Divinópolis might be on the other side of the moon.

GTO—the acronym for Geraldo Teles de Oliveira with which this sculptor signs his carvings—has taken the bus to Belo Horizonte several times to sell a piece to the gift shop that adjoins the state museum of art, or to an enterprising local collector, but aside from these trips he has never left the county in which he was born. When I visited him there in 1975, however, his isolation seemed to be ending dramatically. Showing me a large sculpture of Indians in Colonial times chained to their "cells" in a gold mine, he said the Government of France had commissioned it and had offered to fly him to Paris for its unveiling.[1]

GTO's little house on the Rua Rubi is like every other house in the block except that behind the screen gate to the shallow courtyard one of his characteristic "rings" of small figures is embedded in the wall like a nameplate. Below it, but not visible

[1]This initiative on the part of official France, hitherto indifferent to popular art, may be traced to the influence of André Malraux, General de Gaulle's Minister of Culture. In the same year the French took notice of Haitian popular art for the first time, sponsoring a series of exhibitions and lavishly illustrated books, and Malraux himself paid an official visit to Haiti to study the work of the self-taught painters and sculptors. When I reported GTO's revelation to Lelia Coelho Frota in Rio, that militant friend of the popular artists expressed the belief that Brazil's establishment art critics had alerted the French as part of an effort to "colonize" the "primitives" lest their art overshadow the fading international school.

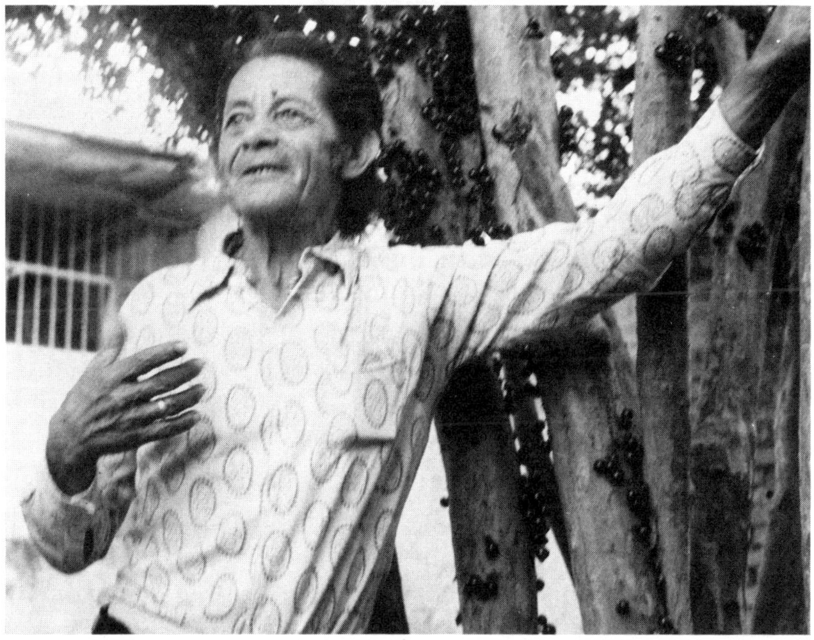

Figure 36. GTO standing by his *jaboticabeira* tree, Divinópolis. Photo: Author.

from the street, is a small replica of GTO's only *un*characteristic piece, a gilded head of Tiradentes, hero of the Brazilian Independence, which the artist was commissioned to make for a square in the village of São João del Rey.

GTO, who was not expecting our visit, came to the door. We found him in because compulsive carvers are always in: it makes them nervous to go far from the workbench and the supply of wood. He is a small bird-like man with deeply creased features under thick black hair. I asked him his height later and he said "1.65 metres" (5 feet, four inches). He introduced us to his wife, and to his son who carves very competently in the paternal style, and then led us into the courtyard where we were invited to pick and eat some of the black "cherries" which grow in clusters directly from the bark of the *jaboticabeiras'* trunk and main branches (Figure 36). Then he took us down the street a couple of blocks to see a sculpture which he had presented recently to the Church of São Bom Jesús where he worships. I had asked to see it because it was carved nine years ago in the first months of his career as a sculptor.

I saw no essential difference in style between this piece and those GTO is doing now. It is in the form of a hinged triptych, and this, in addition to the extraordinary ingenuity with which the figures are deployed in the two small triangles atop the folding wings of the triptych and the large triangular pediment in the center, reminded me instantly of the high-relief stone carvings of the Quattrocento. Not Donatello's or the Della Robbias' for there is nothing of the nascently classical in GTO's figures, but of the Pisan pulpits of the Pisanos which are still close to mediaeval art in the realism with which the Christian legends are depicted. GTO's triptych (Figure 37) suffers not at all by the comparison. The length of the three panels is about 54 inches and the height 36 inches, with an overall depth of two inches. The wood used is red cedar. There are nine divisions (each of the rectangular areas is divided in half). Christ the King, dominating the central pediment, is being honored by a procession of humble worshippers. Some are beating drums and blowing tubas. Some juggle or perform acrobatics. One group in the lower right panel carries a cripple who hopes to be cured. There are angels here and there, and a few detached heads in shallow cylinders. I asked the sculptor what these last signified. "They are sinners, compelled to be without bodies," he explained.

As we stood admiring this remarkable work, *andorinhas* flew through the open windows and circled the cavernous interior of the church. As in the case of José Antônio da Silva's eighteen Stations of the Cross at São José do Rio Preto (see p. 67), tawdry mosaics and carvings adorn the church's central apse; but the parish priest is certainly to be congratulated for having accepted GTO's gift, and for screwing it securely to the wall above the altar in the left transept where it may be seen very well once a vase of paper flowers is removed.

I asked GTO while we were standing there and Bill Negron

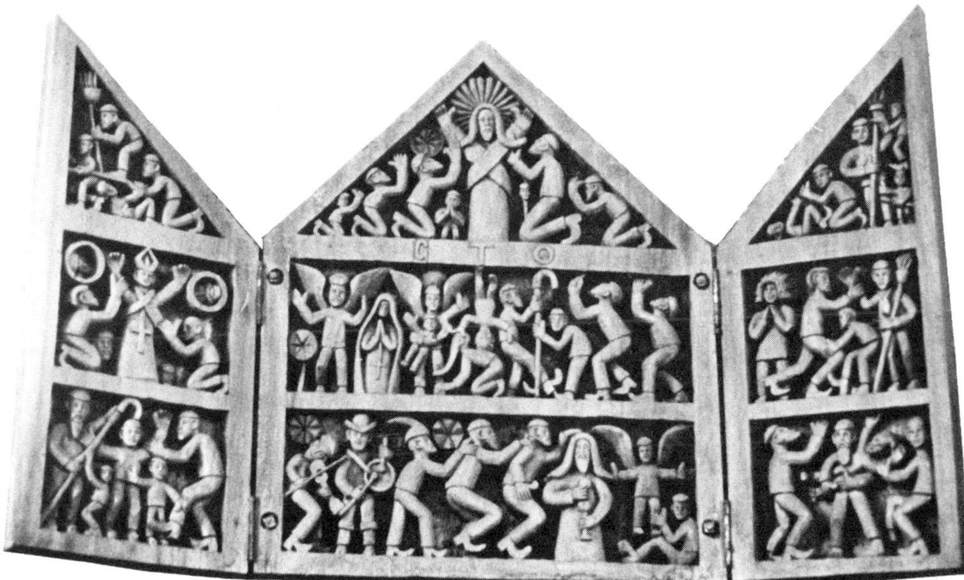

Figure 37. Triptych, Church of São Bom Jesús, Divinópolis. By GTO. Photo: William Negron.

adjusting his tripod, what he did for diversion when not carving.

"Nothing. I am always carving."

"No vices?"

He smiled benignly. "No vices."

Bill reminded him that he chain-smoked cigarettes.

"True."

"No alcohol?"

"Never."

"No women?"

"Only my wife. I'm a devout Christian."

Only a devout Christian could have carved these panels, but

few if any have done so with as much feeling and conviction —and technical mastery—in the last five hundred years.

Back in GTO's home, I asked the sculptor what triggered his career. (Like Louco's and Caboclo's it began in middle age, seemingly without early presentiments or preparation of any kind). It had been eleven years ago, in 1965, when the artist was 52, that he had carved his first piece. He was born January 1, 1913 in Itapeçirica, a small *mineiro* village some 300 kilometers from here on the road to Aleijadinho's Congonhas. His education stopped with the Third Grade of night school in Divinópolis, following which he supported himself as a night guard in the malaria-control section of the Public Health Service, a job which his son Mário now holds.[1] GTO's grandmother was an Amazon Indian, seized in a jungle raid by his grandfather, a slave-dealer and latter-day *bandeirante* who supplied the mines and farms of Minas Gerais with slave labor. Since slavery was abolished by Emperor Dom Pedro II in 1888, this raid must have taken place almost a hundred years ago. GTO's grandfather died in 1925, the artist told me, at the ripe age of 115.[2]

It was in 1965 or 1966—the artist gave me both dates—that GTO had the dream that led to his first sculpture.

"The resulting piece was about four feet high and in the same style as the big sculptures you see here in my workshop, but with the little figures lacking chains—I dreamed the chains later. It was a kind of church, and I sold it almost at once for 300 *cruzeiros* ($30), but to whom I no longer remember. The prices I receive now range all the way from $15 to $50 for the small detached figures to as much as $1500 for the very large assemblages," he added.

"I dreamed the chains, and four months later sculpted them;

[1]Mário, the talented sculptor, is now 33. GTO's only other child, a girl, Marie José, is now 34. GTO and his wife have many grandchildren.

[2]Allowing for a little exaggeration induced by the Brazilian pride in virility-longevity, the great age achieved by GTO's grandfather, and the grandparents of Waldomiro, may be ascribed to the healthy way of life and diet enjoyed by country people in the days before factory labor, the automobile, and processed foods.

but the wheels were my own creativity, discovered here at the workbench. I had been unemployed at the time of my first vision, and I was desperate when God gave me that dream. I had never done any carving—or even simple carpentry—in my life; but God showed me what to do. My vision showed me the complete piece with all its separate parts, so I had only to go to work. I've never stopped working since, except to eat, and sleep, and talk to friends like you; and as I told you in the church, I have no recreations—what would I need them for, with all this work to do?"

I asked GTO if he ever made an preliminary drawings. He showed me figures in a ring drawn with pencil on a circular slab of tree trunk. "Never on paper?" I asked. "Sometimes, but I throw them away.—Wait! here's one you can have," and he reached under the table for an old shoe box, spread out, with a similar drawing in pen. I asked him if he admired the work of any of the other popular sculptors. "Aleijadinho," he said. "But among the living?" He went to get his copy of *7 Artistas Brasileiros e Seu Universo*[1] and pointed to the illustrations of Mestre Dezinho de Valença and Nhō Caboclo. He didn't care for the work of Louco—too "African" perhaps, for GTO has no use for the non-Christian cults. Caboclo, he said, had spent a day with him some time ago, and he had taught the Indian artist how to carve chains without slicing and splicing the wooden links.

We studied the three major pieces in GTO's workshop, each a good example of the three types of sculpture GTO most often makes. The first type, which I will call "GTO No. 1", was represented by a smaller version of the densely populated "ring" in the Belo Horizonte Museum Gift Shop (Figure 38). I photographed the artist holding the smaller piece above his head, silhouetted against one of the white adobe walls (see Frontispiece). What is GTO saying in these rings, whose figures are often so tightly packed inside the circle that some spill over

[1]The handsomely illustrated catalogue of an exhibit mounted by the Ministry of Education and Culture in 1974 at Brasilia.

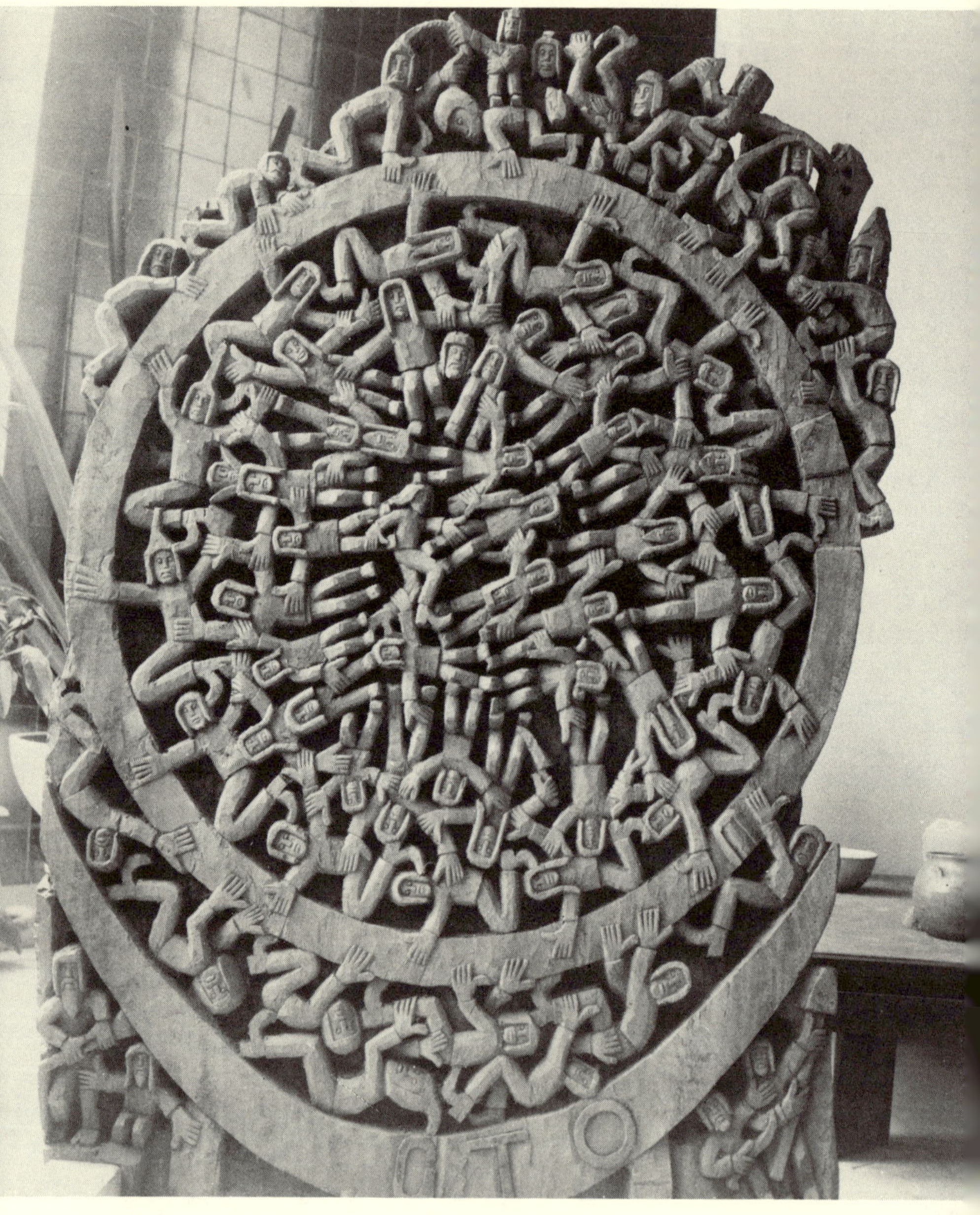

Figure 38. Large Ring. By GTO. Gift Shop, Museu de Artes, Belo Horizonte. Photo: Author.

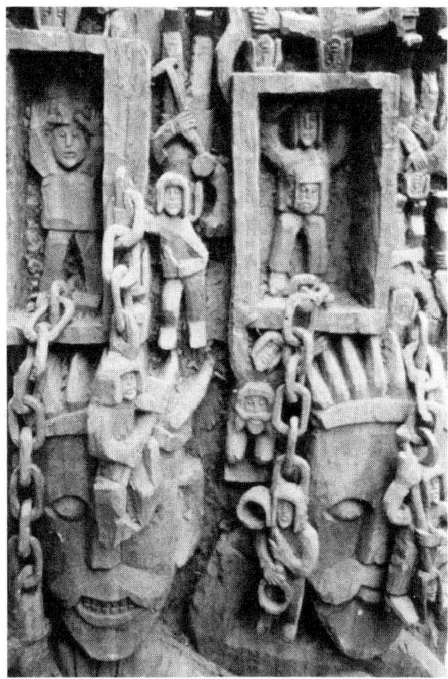

Figure 39. Indian-Slayes Conglomerate (detail). By GTO. Collection: Artist. Photo: William Negron.

the edges where they appear to be hanging on for dear life? Is this our spinning earth? Could he be saying that this is where we're at, for better or worse, and that those who refuse to fit in or accommodate themselves to the world's fragile environment will lose their sense of belonging anywhere? Or is he saying that the cycle of birth, life, death, endlessly repeats itself and that the only meaning is in the perfection of the pattern? Or is he unconsciously confirming Einstein—demonstrating that "up" and "down" depend upon the Hypothetical Observor's position and have as little ultimate meaning as time? Or—?

The "scenario" of "GTO No. 2" seems more down to earth. An Indian "King" or "Queen" presides over the tribe reduced to slavery by the Portuguese colonizer (Detail Figure 39). But again, the meaning is elusive, having as little to do with the "realities" of "history" in this case, as "GTO No. 1" has to do with circus acrobatics. Clearly the Chief is God for he alone is not chained to his habitat. But why are the ordinary mortals not only chained but given such dimensions that they will fit in their cells only if stuffed or jammed in sidewise? The mind of such a "Gothic" painter of the Quattrocento as Sassetta would *know* what GTO "knows," and what is for us only guesswork. Which is not to maintain that Sassetta or GTO could *say* what they know, except through their art.

"GTO No. 3," the conglomerate with moving parts that doubles as a musical instrument, is the most poetic and mysterious of GTO's creations. He has made several of these "*trapizongas,*" as he calls them, in the course of his eleven-year career, and we were fortunate in finding one, commissioned and almost finished, in the Divinópolis workshop.

Without a photograph (Figure 40) the piece would be difficult to describe. Basically, there are seven upright figures, sixteen inches high—Indians probably, for their headgear is plumed, with hinged arms and legs permitting some movement. They are attached at their backs to vertical rods with cams. These cams are geared to seven pieces of wood protruding from a horizontal camshaft—the shaft itself carved intricately with figures in low relief. When the camshaft, or axle, is rotated by means of two solid wooden wheels with a small handle on one of them, the seven "Indians" dance up and down, but in sequence not in unison, with their hinged arms flapping. The axle, three or four feet long, is supported by uprights at either end against the wheels, and planted in a platform resting on the floor. The platform also supports the higher uprights in the rear which keep the seven figures in their fixed positions. Leather straps connecting the camshaft to the insides of the wheels facilitate the motion of the mechanism which might otherwise stall or jam.

"It's a musical instrument," GTO exclaimed excitedly as he turned the crank to start the seven figures dancing wildly. "It sings the song of the wood with seven distinct notes, all harmonized perfectly… you hear it?"

Figure 40. *Trapizonga.* By GTO. Collection: Artist. Photo: William Negr

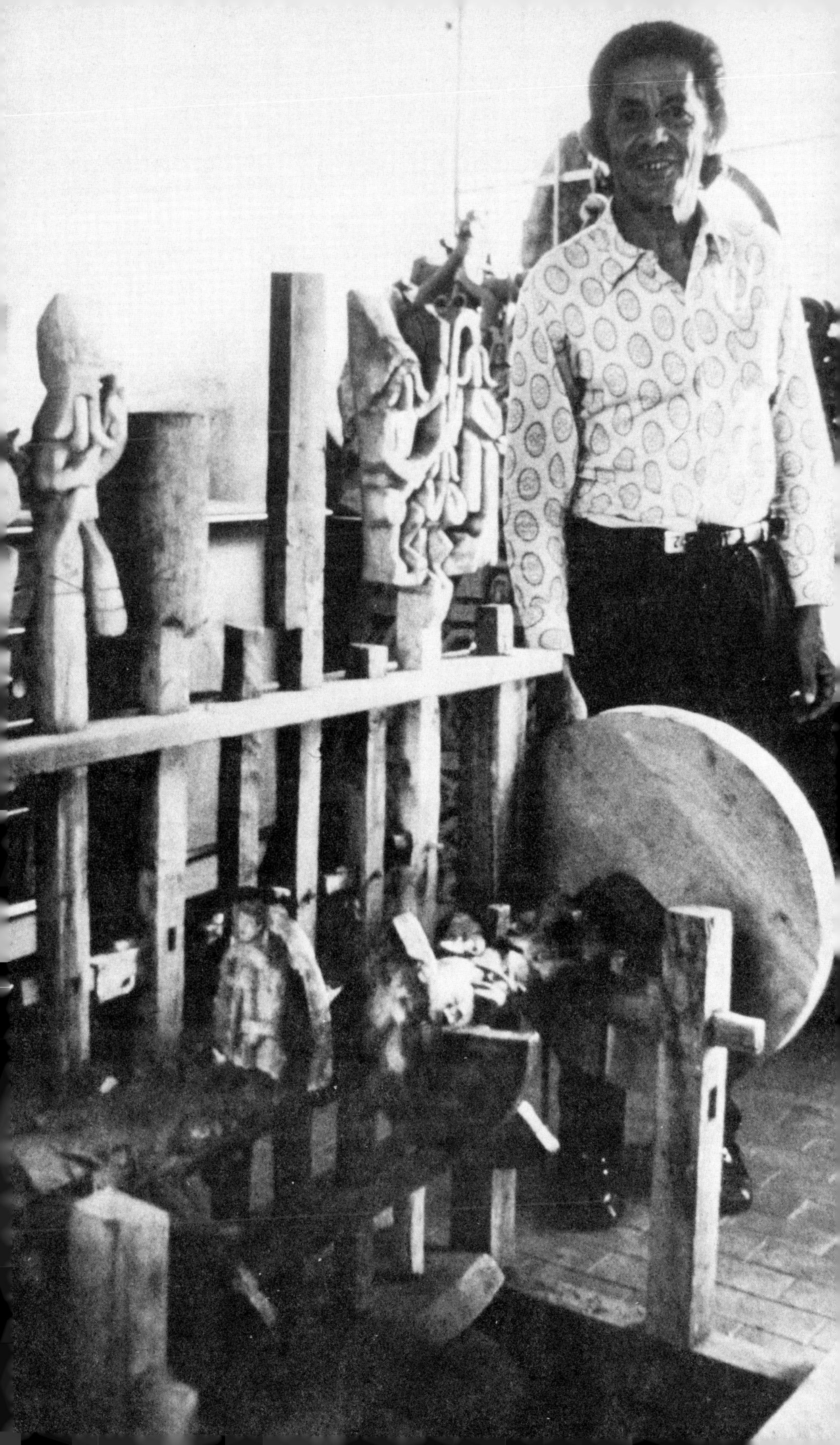

We heard the wood creak, rattle and shriek, but the "music" was for GTO's ears alone, conveyed to us only by the visual poetry of this great artist's invention. Could it be a dance of death, a tarantella of devils, as Bill suggested later? Or another symbolic simulacrum of the world, with humanity activated briefly and violently but advancing nowhere?

I asked GTO where he got the idea for this third type of sculpture. From ancient devices, he told me, once used in the gold mines of Minas Gerais (the state's name means General Mines) to separate the ore from the slag. Was there a connection, I wondered, with Nhō Caboclo's "mobiles" of gyrating Indians? Could Caboclo have seen one of these mysterious "machines" on that unexplained visit to Divinópolis some years ago? Or did their common heritage as Indians lead to similar solutions of making sculpture more life-like?

I had seen one other example of mobility in popular sculpture in Brazil. It was a ceramic or moulded clay "conglomerate" of figurines in the collection of Dona Lilli Correia de Araujo at the Pousa Chico Rey in Ouro Prêto, the colonial capital of Minas Gerais. It represented the martyrdom of Tiradentes, and although the little figures surrounding the gallows were fixed to their base, the hero of the Brazilian Independence hung by a string from the gibbet, swaying slightly in the breeze (Figure 40 A). Dona Lilli told me that Levy José Martins the folk artist who had made it some years ago, lived in Diamantina, so I went to that exquisite hill town in the northwest part of the state to find him.

Lévy, sadly, had died the year before, and not a single example of his work was to be found in Diamantina. His widow told us that she had been obliged to sell all of her husband's remaining pieces for a few *cruzeiros* to buy the tiny shack and garden which they had been renting and which is now the old lady's only source of livelihood. As we sat with her (as with GTO) under a bountiful *jaboticabeira* picking black cherries, the same story, by now familiar, unfolded. Lévy, like all the others, had been a late bloomer. Before his death in 1972 at the age of 78, he

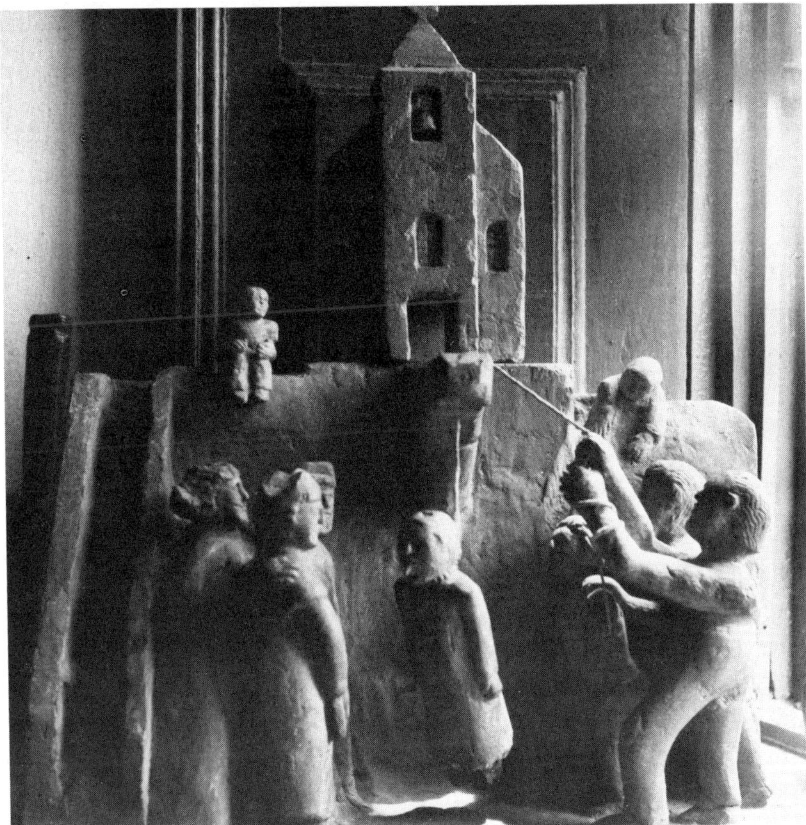

Figure 40A. The Martyrdom of Tiradentes. By Lévy. Collection: Lilli Correia de Araujo, Ouro Prêto. Photo: Author.

had made a living as an automobile mechanic, and before that as a cutter of stones from which diamonds are extracted. This craft, when he began making sculpture four years before his death, stood him in good stead. He knew all about working soapstone with a chisel. But the originality of his style and his choice of subjects insured that the establishments, local and national, would spurn him. His most elaborate piece showed a tree filled with monkeys engaged in a suicidal scramble for power. In another, a priestly devil is pushing an unwilling husband into marriage with his bride. The wife of a doctor in Diamantina who had admired Lévy's work, made us a drawing of the Monkey

Tree, in which the monkey reaching for the empty "throne" at the top is "shooting" those who dangle by their tails from the lower branches. She claimed to have seen a similar conglomerate by GTO in the collection of the director of the Catholic Marilles Theater in Belo Horizonte. Lévy, she added, carved so many pieces involving "devils" that the Bishop of Diamantina decided he must either be dealing in "black magic" or have "Communist affiliations"! When this intelligence was duly circulated, Lejzojbgzwas avoided like the plague, his meager income depending thenceforth entirely on visiting tourists.

We said goodbye to GTO reluctantly. Ever smiling, he shook hands with us; but looking back from the door, we could see him whittling away in exactly the same position as we had found him when entering.

I reflected once more on the "meaning" of GTO's world, though in a way it's absurd to do more than *enjoy* such art with the same open-minded reverence that went into its creation. On the surface, of course, GTO is only depicting the visible world, and the exploitation of the Indian as he had no doubt heard his grandfather describe it. But as he says himself, he doesn't really know *why* he suddenly began to carve chained figures and the like. His visions directed him to. So perhaps the important lesson is to be receptive to visions.

Part III:

ENTERTAINERS AND EXPLORERS

As modern art forges ahead, it seems to become more and more indifferent to what art signified, whether deliberately or not, during untold ages: a form of man's awareness of the world...Is not our art, born of a cleavage of man's consciousness, tending to "possess" no more than its private kingdom–that of painting?

—André Malraux

The abstract is not life and everywhere draws out its contradictions. You can refute Hegel but not the Saint or the Song of Sixpence.

—W. B. Yeats

GTO and Nhô Caboclo create poetry of motion; but their figures move, like a composer's notes, within fixed limits. The sovereign artist makes his own laws, deciding how we are to look at his world. But within that larger frame of independence, some are indifferent to tradition; some remake it in their own image; and others consciously attempt a breakthrough from here and now. Thus, among the six artists we have been dealing with so far, GTO and Caboclo are inventive revolutionaries; Djanira a popular classicist; Louco and José Antônio da Silva expressionists working with traditional limits; and Waldomiro a transitional figure driven by his demons to release archetypal images, but ambitious to create out of them a new art with world-wide antecedents.

Most of the artists now to be considered share Waldomiro's ambitions, moving in the art-conscious colonies of Rio and São Paulo. Many of them, like that painter, were born in the Northeast. The best of them have achieved original and consistent styles. A few won fame when popular art was not a dirty word or a battle cry, and live comfortably on their reputations, repeating themselves, or sometimes not bothering to paint at all.

CASSIO M'BOY

There was a time—after the eclipse of Heitor Dos Prazeres and the establishment's brush-off of José Antônio da Silva—when Cassio was considered *the* "Brazilian primitive." His paintings date from that period, and eleven were reproduced in color in a handsome catalogue, presented by the Associação Brasileira de Folclôre and published by the São Paulo State Secretariat of Culture, Exports and Tourism. It is said that Cassio repaints a picture from that period when he needs money, and the prices he receives for them are as high as the quality is perfunctory. Judging by the catalogue, it was not always so; and even the repeats still bear traces of the poetic imagination with which Cassio interpreted the old legends. That imagination is now verbalized, but in the fantasies of Cassio's running monologue are embedded gemstones of the true Brazil.

The word 'M'Boy' in his painter's-name, Cassio once told me, means 'cobra' in Tupi-Guarani[1] but he adopted it for its aptness in describing the serpentine river near his birthplace, Embú, which the Indians pronounced 'M'Boy'. (Embú in the 'Sixties became an artists' colony, a sort of Montparnasse or Greenwich Village on the outskirts of São Paulo.) Cassio adopted the name, he added, because his aunt, the Baroness Jaguará, told him not to soil the family name by being an artist.

Lion-maned, flabby, gay, and invariably sporting no more

[1]There are no cobras in South America, though the coral snake resembles them. Tupi-Guarani was the principal Indian language along the Atlantic coast when the Portuguese arrived in 1500.

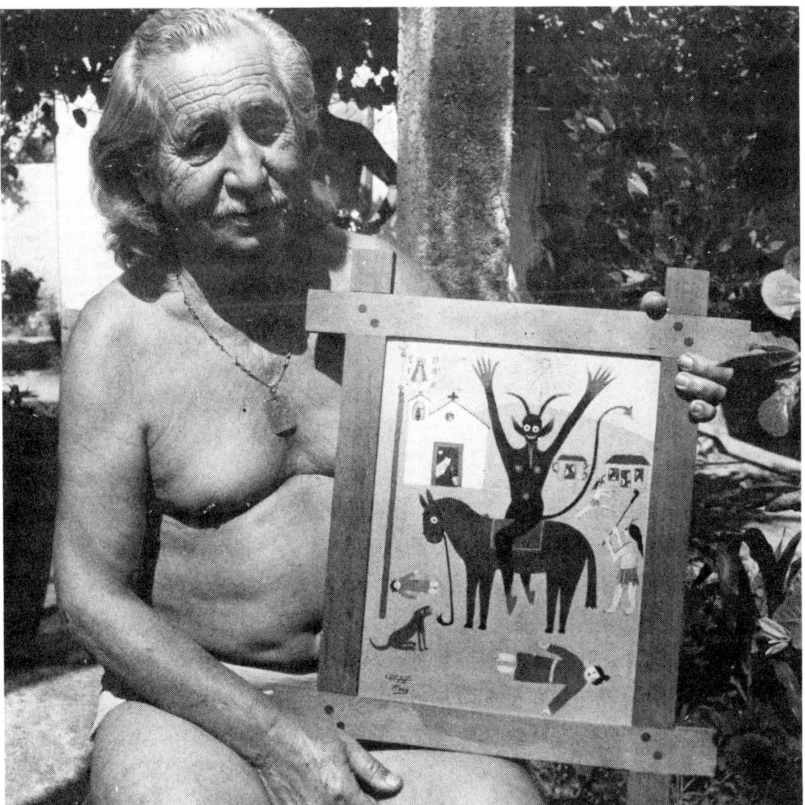

Figure 41. Cassio M'Boy holding one of his paintings, São Paulo. Photo: Author.

than a pair of yellow, bikini-style shorts, the artist receives visitors in the sun-splashed grape arbor of his comfortable middle-class home—and begins talking (Figure 41). I asked him what saint was represented in a picture that stood on an easel, and why she was wearing a Star of David on her necklace.

"She is Santa Lúcia," he explained, "and she came to me in a dream at three in the morning. You notice her bloody eyes on the golden plate she holds? She was blinded with a red-hot poker; but since a miracle restored them, she has another O.K. set in her head, as you can see. The star is a matter of syncretism. São Paulo was settled by Jews in 1544. So I am one, though of course I have Indian and African blood too like all *paulistas*. The

Jews had been persecuted by the Inquisition in Santos so they came to this village. Here, surrounded by Indians, they integrated and formed a new culture called Caipira. The symbolism in my pictures expresses this *branco-indio-prêto* racial amalgam.

"I was self-taught," he went on, "not only in painting, but in musical composition, violin-playing, and poetry, in all of which I excelled. In 1929 I committed intellectual suicide by rejecting the academic-modernist cannons of art. Later, in Paris[1] in 1940, I decided to be a primitive and give Brazil an art wholly Brazilian. You can see the result."

He pointed with a sweep of his hand to the prototypes of his paintings on the walls, each of them framed in four ugly strips of varnished wood, crossed at the corners. On a table was a collection of his old catalogues, a pile of press-clippings, and a block of 1970 Brazilian stamps featuring his "St. Gabriel."

"They paid you rights of reproduction, Cassio?"

"They didn't ask permission to use it. In fact, I had to buy this block after a friend showed me one on a letter."

"I have two personalities," he rambled on, "gentleman farmer and aristocrat, and I feel comfortable in both. The most cultured men in the world, including Brazil's great poet Cassiano Ricardez, call me the most universal fountainhead of Brazilian art. Before me, Brazilians made only imitations of other arts. I created the original imagery of Brazilian history and legend."

I asked him if he remembered William Krauss, an American friend who had sent me photographs of Cassio's pictures in the early 'Fifties when I was living in Haiti. He didn't remember, but he showed me a reproduction of a picture by Toussaint Auguste.

"You like Haitian painting, Cassio?"

"Not especially."

"Mexican?"

[1]On an another occasion Cassio denied that he had ever been abroad, and denied more vehemently that he had been influenced by the Surrealists.

"Too French-influenced."

"Portinari?"

"Out of Picasso. I wanted to create an art having nothing to do with Europe."

"But it has something to do with the *turcos,* the Middle East and India, hasn't it?"

"Yes. And Japan—because the Indians came from Japan, just as the Jews came from Syria, and I have both bloods in my veins. Cassio," he continued, speaking of himself in the third person as he usually does, "is the enemy of the Bienal and all it stands for. The artists it promotes are all little Europeans, from Portinari on down."

"Then you must like José Antônio da Silva."

"The best! He is a true *caipira* like Cassio. Brazilians, like Americans, are ashamed of their racial origins. They like to think of themselves as pure Portuguese—an absurdity."

JÚLIO MARTINS DA SILVA

In his book about the Brazilian aboriginals of the Mato Grosso and the Amazon watershed,[1] Claude Lévi-Strauss, with that degree of romanticism permitted to social anthropologists, describes the harmonious life in the elliptical community dwellings divided down the middle to prevent incestuous breeding, and how the Indians lost that harmony as soon as the Iberian conquerors arrived and resettled them in villages with grid-like plans. Rio de Janeiro, similarly was a place of harmonious family living and homogeneous architecture at the turn of the century when Júlio Martins da Silva began to look about him and store up those memories he would later paint. There were no automobiles, no traffic, no pollution—and no rickety slums, for the village poor had not yet so increased in numbers, thanks to

[1]*Tristes Tropiques:* An Anthropological Study of Primitive Societies in Brazil. New York: Atheneum, 1964. Original French edition, 1955.

medical and sanitary improvements, that they were obliged to descend upon the cities in hordes. The spacious parks were laced with bridle paths. And there were gardens dotted with statuary and those miniature "crystal palaces" that the Emperor Dom Pedro II had admired during his extensive travels abroad in Victorian England, the Continent and the United States Centennial Exposition (Color Plate 4A).

In his seventies and eighties, Júlio remembered this Rio in the same way that Philomé Obin remembered the Cap Haïtien of the parasolled mulatto élite in their cabriolets driven by black coachmen, and the *cacos* guerillas riding wildly over the red Hyppolite Bridge; or Henri Rousseau the tropical jungles of his fantasy-journey to Mexico; or Horace Pippin the drawing rooms of the great ladies along Philadelphia's Main Line, as glimpsed in awe through the eyes of a black janitor.

Júlio had been born in Icarai, now a part of the city of Niteroi across Guanabara Bay from Rio, in 1893. He didn't paint until he was 50. He supported himself and his family, after moving to Rio when he was 18, as hod-carrier, delivery man, grocery clerk and cook. Ah! those ineffable birthday- and wedding-cakes of the rich with their pink and white tracery, their little "kings" and "queens" and "fairies" posturing on top, and their scattered "snow" sparkling with red and green flecks of crystal candy. How effectively he would use them!

Júlio's grandfather had been a slave. His father, who died when Júlio was seven, took him on walks through the Botanical Gardens, to the Quinta de Bõa Vista where the Emperor had lived, and once even to a farm out of town—the subject of his first picture. At first he had given these pictures, expressing his yearning for the countryside he would never know, to anyone who asked for one. He showed five of them, framed and priced at 3 *cruzeiros* (30c) each, in a Rio boutique, but none was bought. Fortunately Lélia Coelho Frota saw them and went at once to see him in the suburban *favela* called Coelho Neto where he then lived. It was 1964 and Júlio's career as a popular artist had begun. The perceptive young critic showed his pictures later to

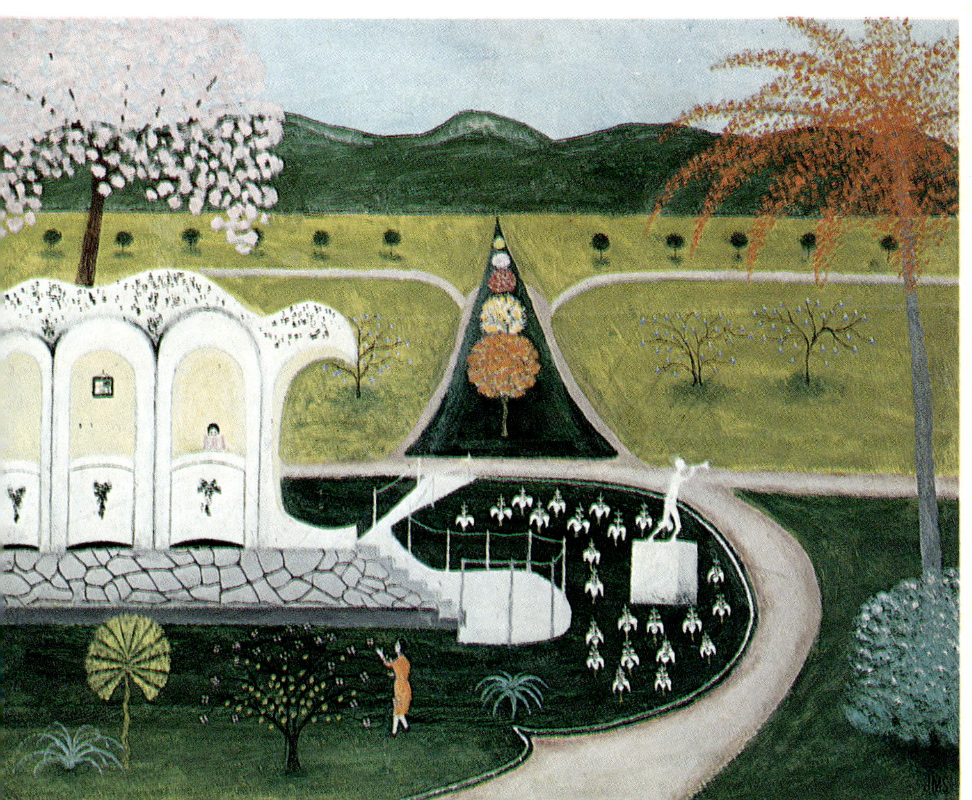

A. Crystal Palace. By Julio Martins da Silva. Collection: Author. Photo: Manu Sassoonian.

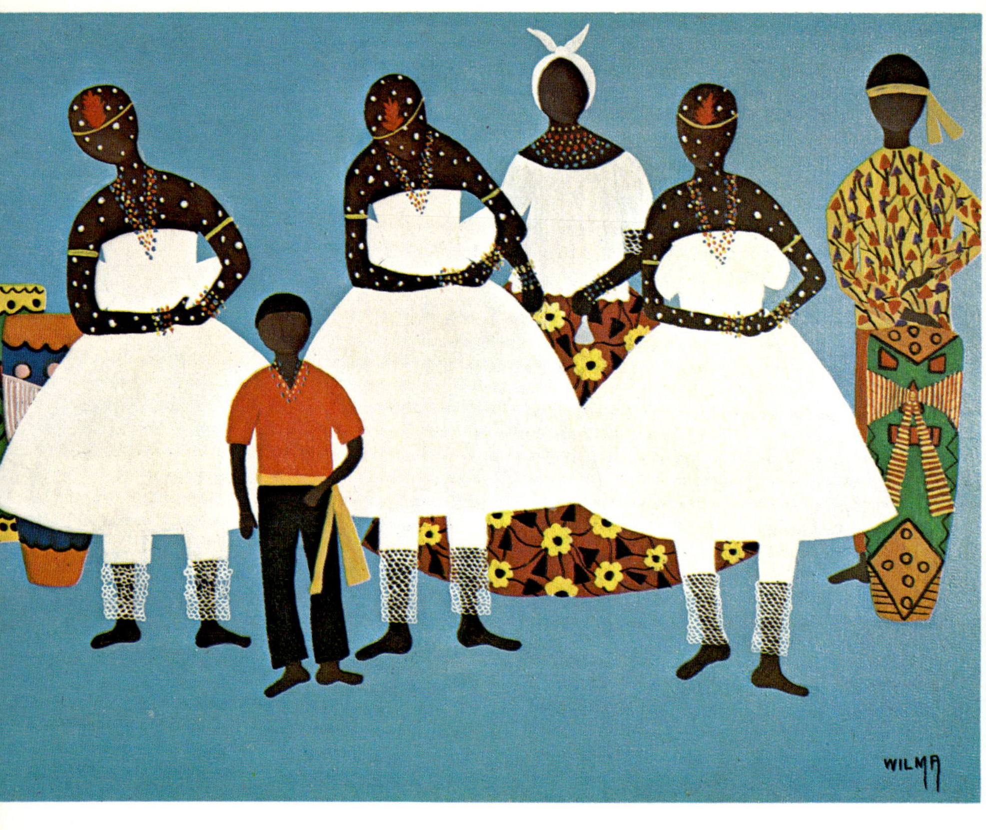

B. Masked Figures in *Candomblé*. By Wilma. Collection: Dr. and Mrs. Ron Kessler, Saddle River, New Jersey. Photo: Manu Sassoonian.

C. Sailor's Delight. By Francisco V. da Silva. Collection: Author. Photo: Manu Sassoonian.

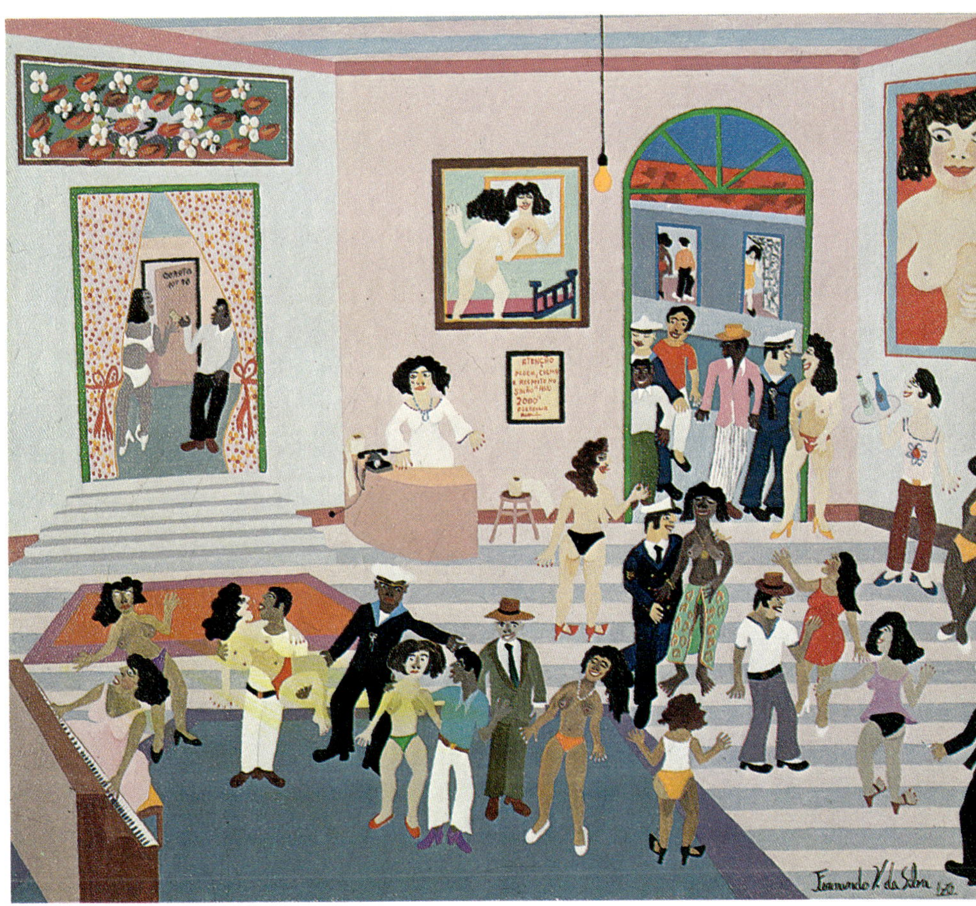

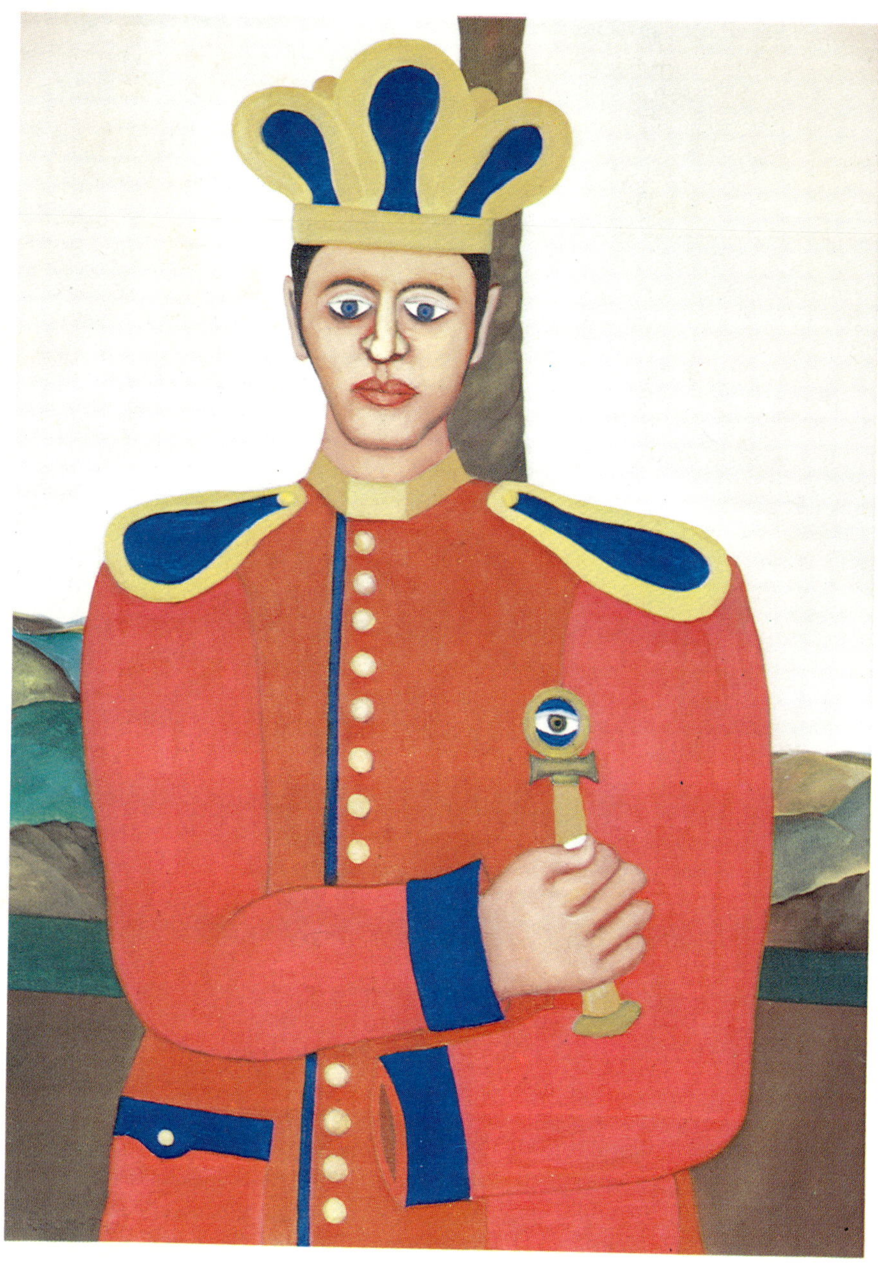

D. The King and Eye. By Gerson de Souza. Collection: Author. Photo: Manu Sassoonian.

Maria Elisa Carrazzoni, the Director of the Museu Nacional de Bellas Artes under whom she worked, and in 1971 the museum bought three of his pictures. In 1975 the same Rio museum gave Júlio a one-man retrospective.

One of the pictures in this exhibit was called "A Dialogue between Roses and Orange Blossoms" and was accompanied by the following poem in the artist's hand. Translated roughly, it goes:

> I am a rose, sweet and proud.
> I dress myself in beautiful colors,
> And among the famous flowers
> I'm considered the loveliest.
>
> Since always first in house or garden,
> First to be smelled, first to be touched,
> It is my due to live among lovers
> Surrounded by love.
>
> And I am the orange blossom
> Pledged to the future;
> No queen among flowers, but first to be touched
> When blossoms are sprinkled ahead of the bride.
>
> I have my place,
> Not renowned among lovers,
> But from my seed
> The fruit is born.

There were people going about their business in another picture, a night piece with a velvety black sky in which the stars and moon are neatly placed, and a jaguar peeps from the trees. Lélia Coelho came up to us as we were admiring it and remarked: "Those cold people no longer know how to look at poetry by moonlight, but the jaguar does."

She introduced us to the artist (Figure 42), who showed his 80 years only in his difficulty in rising from the chair without assistance. His shiny black head is closely shaved. His gaze is very alert, and he is articulate. He walked with us to show us a picture of flowers being shot out of a cannon at a wedding ceremony. "It is my imagining," he said. "Marriage is better than war, don't you agree?" We agreed. And he moved to another picture, an elaborate castle filling an island in a small lake. Lélia said the castle was from a postcard someone had sent Júlio from Portugal showing the Fifteenth Century Tower of Belém.

The most arresting picture in the show was titled "Borboletta" (Figure 43). A stunning green butterfly has just alighted on the steps of a palace it completely dwarfs—dominating, in fact, the center of the picture. Lélia had already explained: "He's bringing the jungle to a human level, domesticating it." I asked Júlio why he had painted the insect so large. "To fill the composition." Both explanations made sense. But the artist was more concerned to give us the scenario of the three tiny girls leaving from the balconies, and the man with the briefcase on the garden path. "He loves the girl above him. The second girl is writing a love letter. But you notice how sad the third girl looks? She wants to be loved but no one loves her."

"Júlio has always been a devout Baptist," Lélia told us. "His pastor is amazed that people buy his 'child-like' paintings, but the pastor is a good man; he always attends Júlio's shows, and he hangs his pictures in his religious festivals. So Júlio is integrated very well in his community. His symbolism is always religious, whether he knows it or not."

Where people appear in his pictures, they are of Liliputian dimensions. That, as in the pictures of the Nicaraguan Asîlia Guillén, explains part of their charm. But in a picture with only one tiny fruit-picker the poetry is conveyed by the fairy-like architecture, the delicate tracery of trees and formal gardens, the gesturing enigmatic sculpture, and the tiny bits of glittering tinsel which the artist mixes with his paints from time to time to give an added iridescence. Moreover the pictures are invariably

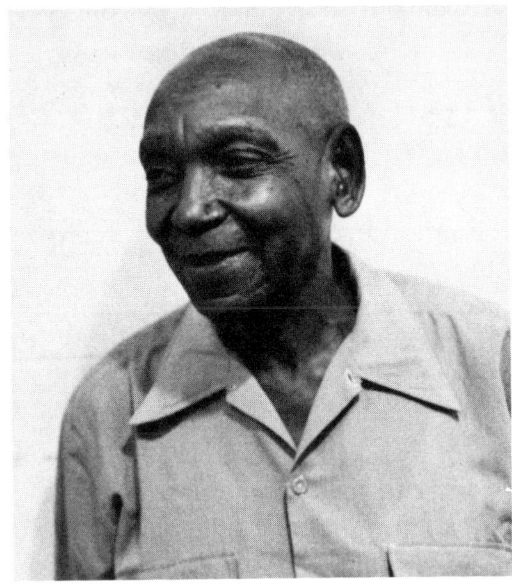

Figure 42. Júlio Martins da Silva at his 1975 exhibition. Photo: William Negron.

Figure 43. (below) *Borboletta* (The Butterfly.) By Júlio Martins da Silva. Photo: William Negron.

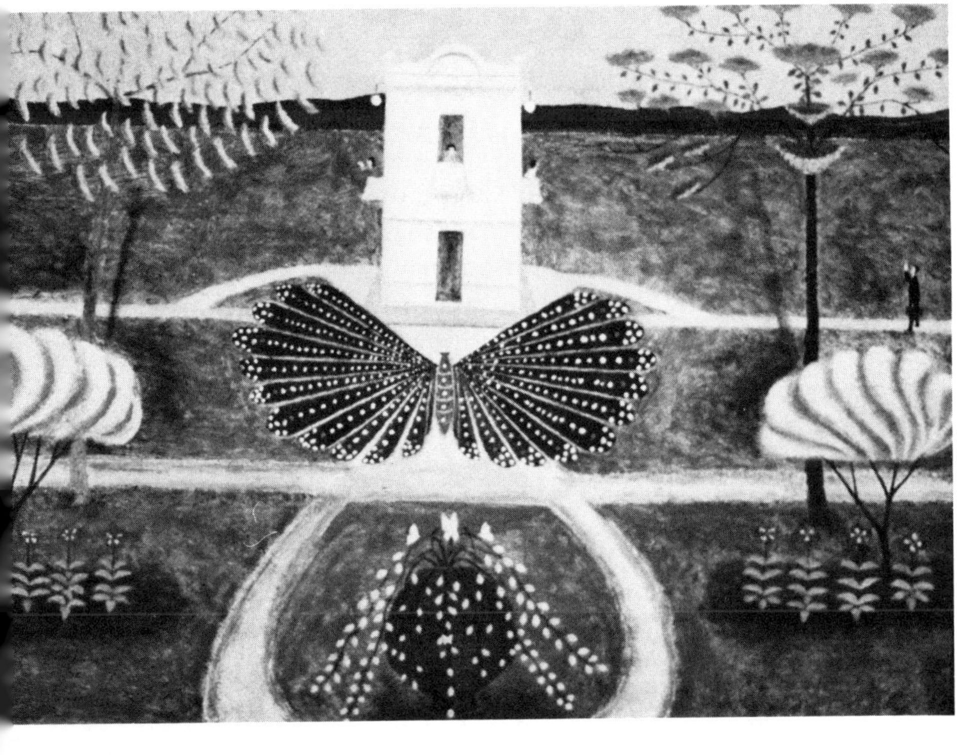

so well put together that, as Bill Negron remarked, "They'd work almost as well if hung upside down."

RAIMUNDO DE OLIVEIRA AND CHICO DA SILVA

Raimundo de Oliveira and Chico da Silva were the two most "Indian" of the popular painters in the 'Fifties and 'Sixties, and received a degree of recognition in the museums and among Brazilian collectors.

Raimundon a Bahian, was probably not an Indian or a *caboclo* at all, but a middle-class eccentric of great talent who developed a very personal style and never varied it. He committed suicide some time in the early 'Seventies, but not before making some splended engravings on Biblical subjects which Julio Pacello, the São Pàulo publisher of limited editions, brought out sumptuously. Raimundo's characteristic figures are little gnomes or dwarfs with large heads, usually seen in profile, prowling through an emerald-ruby twilight (Figure 44).

Chico da Silva is a *caboclo* who still lives in Pirambú, one of the poorest districts of Fortaleza, an Atlantic port city north of Recife in the state of Ceará. He was born in Acre on the Peruvian border in 1928 of a Peruvian mother and father from Ceará. He was discovered in 1943 by Jean Pierre Chabloz, a French piano repairman in Fortaleza, already scratching out his typical ghost ships, jungle dragons and spectral fish. The Frenchman took these pictures in chalk, charcoal and red clay to Rio, and then to Paris. Chico had some early recognition in both capitals, and then was forgotten.

"I became a shoemaker," the artist told a Brazilian reporter recently, "and also a master in oxygen and carburate, boat watchman, skindiver familiar with all underwater creatures, umbrella repairman, barber and sailor. And then in Salvador I met my *baiana* wife who sold *acarajé* (a sweet) and we had twelve children, five of whom are still alive and painting, but only Chico da Silva paints like me."

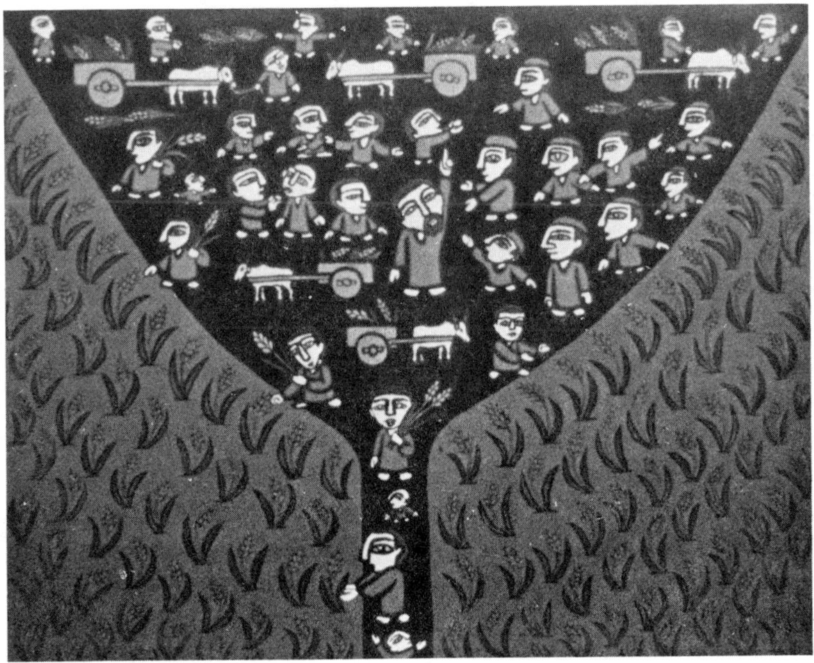

Figure 44. Harvest Tree. By Raimundo da Oliveira. Collection: Ernest Wolf, São Paulo.

The artist was no doubt defending himself against the widespread suspicion that his recent pictures, which flood the tourist shops from Fortaleza to São Paulo are turned out in a "factory" where even his thumbprint and signature with the reversed 'd' and 'S' are mimicked by assistants.[1] But unfortunately the poor

[1]The well-known Haitian popular artist, Préfèt Duffaut of Jacmel, suffered the same fate, painting imaginatively and with brilliant precision when he was an illiterate peasant, then repeating himself *ad nauseam* when he moved to the capital, lived it up, and sold pictures effortlessly to tourists without descrimination. See *The Miracle of Haitian Art*, op. cit. p. 75.

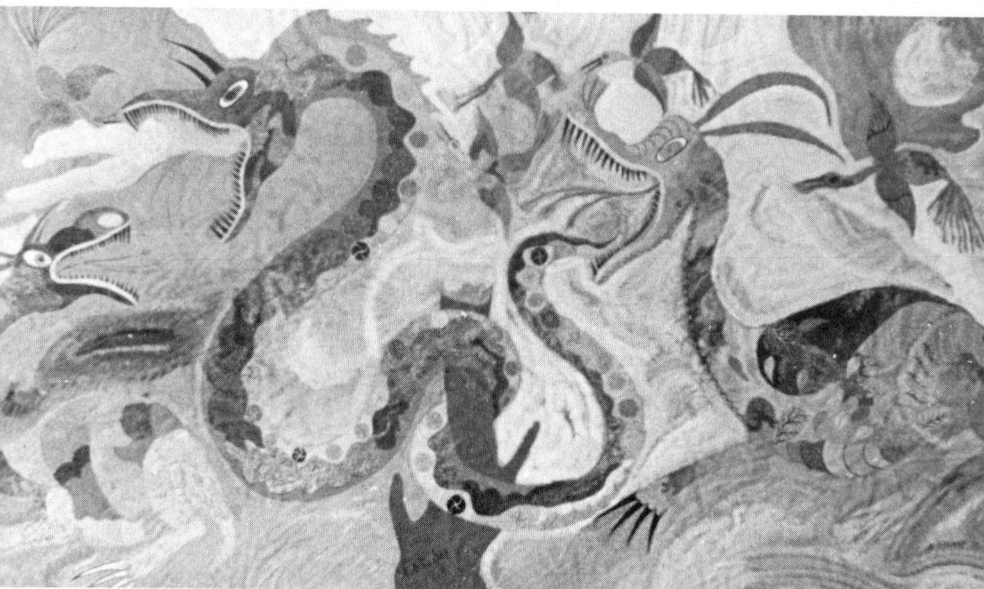

Figure 45. Sea Creatures. By Chico da Silva. Grande Hotel, Recife. Photo: Manu Sassoonian.

quality of these pictures lead one to presume that it is true. How well Chico could paint his jungle fantasies a decade or two ago when he exercised the great care which this painstaking kind of "X-ray" illumination requires, may be seen in the huge (60″ x 36″) picture of fish which hangs in the dining alcove of the Hotel Grande in Recife (Figure 45).

MANEZINHO ARAUJO

A similar fate has overtaken Manoel ('Manezinho') Araujo, a Northeasterner who was born in Cabo, Pernambuco, twenty minutes from downtown Recife, in 1910, and now lives in São Paulo. For most of his life Manezinho was a successful popular composer and singer in the nightclubs. He showed me a picture of himself taken in the 'Thirties, chubby, making faces in a pork-pie hat, like a vaudeville song-and-dance man. Fifteen years ago in Rio, inspired by the renown of popular-composer

Heitor Dos Prazeres, he began to paint. "I looked at a picture by another self-taught artist and decided I could do better." Those early paintings are scenes of *candomblé* and *macumba* for the most part, each tiny figure rendered with immaculate precision. But Manezinho, though he made no effort to vary or surpass this charming formula which began to bring him high prices in the chic galleries of Rio and São Paulo, soon became ambitious to join the ranks of the "modern artists."

I asked him for the scenario of just such a painting—hands emerging from holes in the ground holding plates containing "eyes." I was reminded of Cassio's picture, except that in this case the bloody "eyes" looked like fried eggs, sunnyside-up. "Santa Lúcia," Manezinho explained, "is the protector of sight." And there was another such pseudo-surrealist painting of a huge veined leaf protruding obtrusively into a landscape with a farmer placed artfully in the foreground.

One painting did intrigue me, flowers and leaves in yellow *impasto* on the front door of the artist's apartment, curving around the peep-hole and buzzer, with these serving as the flowers' pistils (Figure 46). Manezinho smiled deprecatingly and

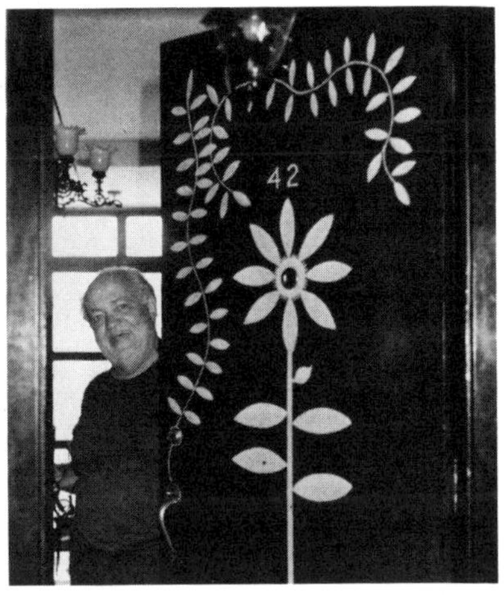

Figure 46. Manezinho at the door of his São Paulo apartment-studio. Photo: Manu Sassoonian.

apologized for it. He is a short, fat man with stubby pepper-and-salt beard on his double chin. Wearing slacks and a T-shirt, he moves about his sunny studio like a shopkeeper displaying his wares. Jars and tubes of paint are neatly arranged on tilted trays. Primed canvases are stacked behind sliding panels. His output last year, he said, was 300 pictures. His wife executes competent tapestries after his designs and sells them in the $500-$600 range. His own small paintings bring more. And his serigraphs sell for as much as a $100 apiece. Seeing a reproduction of one of Djanira's paintings on the wall, I asked Manezinho whether he had borrowed from her the convention of painting figures in *candomblés* with featureless faces. He said that he had arrived at it independently. "I am no longer a primitive," he added proudly, "but I paint like no one else in the world."

TERCILIANO DOMINGOS

Like Djanira, Terciliano is essentially a decorative painter. But the forms of both artists are firmly rooted in the Brazilian scene. They are what matters, the content. Both artists have an unerring eye for the grace and gesture of simple, unaffected people; and both are brilliant colorists. Neither artist gives form to feelings, neuroses or mystical visions.

Terciliano, tall, wiry, black with an Afro (Figure 47) was born in Salvador in 1939, and began painting there in 1963. He had a show that year at the Galeria Vermón, and one at the Galeria Itau in São Paulo in 1974. In the foreword to the earlier show, the *baiano* novelist Jorge Amado wrote: "*Candomblé* and its *orixás* give Terciliano his impressions of Bahia where color and mystery merge. He had them in his blood. When he paints, it's like a ritual obligation. But the hard life of the people as well as Bahia's ritualism are reflected in his art. There is nothing forced or false in Terciliano, so he belongs with such other great Bahian primitives as Willys, Pedroso, Ana Lúcia, Louco and Cardoso e Silva."

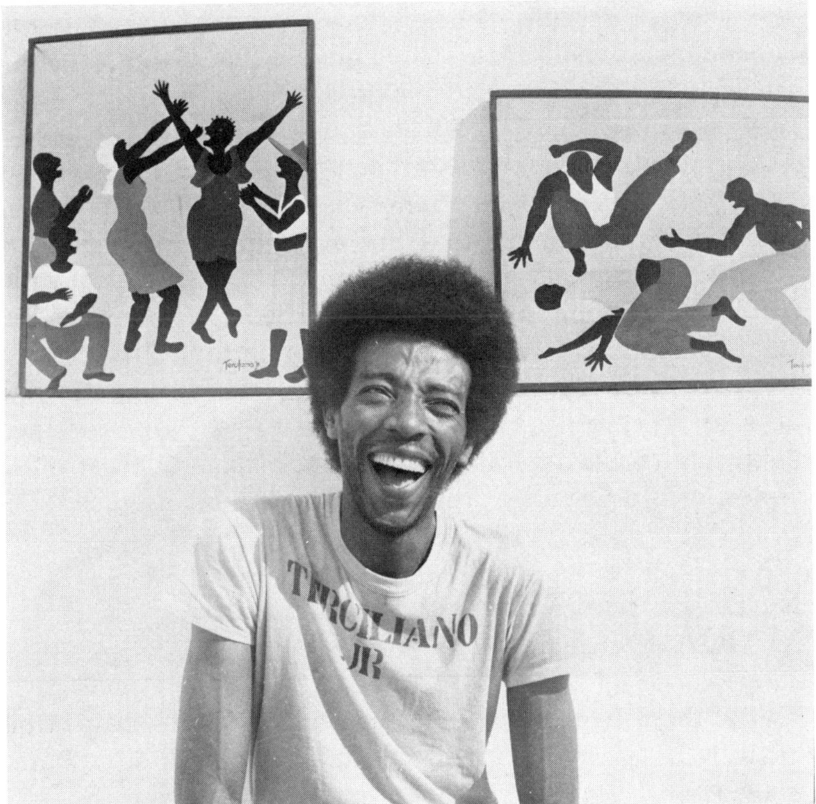

Figure 47. Terciliano with two of his paintings, São Paulo. Photo: William Negron.

If a dangerous facility was apparent in Terciliano's paintings in those early days, Amado was too kind to mention it. For the silhouette has become Terciliano's trademark. When his *capoeira* dancers,[1] fishermen, or masked participants in *candomblé* are depicted starkly against a neutral background (see Figure 47) the images are compelling. But recently Terciliano has taken to decking his figures in elaborate necklaces and headgear, presenting them in pairs or in quartets, and the result is sometimes a formula closer to décor or fashion layout than to painting.

[1]A Bahian popular dance, *capoeira* derives from a slave technique of disarming oppressors with the feet.

Whether Terciliano manages to escape from this trap will depend on his character and ambition. He has the gift. And an intellectual curiosity to match the range of his talents. He had a brief career as an actor in Rio, appearing in Brazilian versions of *Alice in Wonderland* and *Hair*. (When he asked his mother what she'd think if he copied a current fad and painted his hair white, she said: "You want to look like a *negative?*) He played his *berimbau* for us, and remarked casually that he was already the father of five children, though unmarried. "I got them," he laughed, "before TV became popular in Salvador."

As we got up to take leave of him in his São Paulo apartment, he said: "There's a question I'd like to ask you. Is James Baldwin's racism typical of black intellectuals in the United States, or is it just a by-product of his neurotic personality?"

ROSINA BECKER DO VALLE AND MARIA LACERDA

Why these two educated women of the middle class paint "naively" is less important than the fact that they do so enchantingly.

Rosina Becker has been painting minutely detailed scenes of Brazilian life (Figure 48), and still lifes, for a long time, and she is represented in several museum collections. Born in 1914, she lives with her husband, one of their four children, a Pekingese, and two caged mastiffs in an apartment in the Granja section of Rio, where I visited her. Her father made jewelry settings and this may have given her the taste for dense floral backgrounds and tiled interiors. While in school she made copies of famous paintings. "When they were perfect copies," she told me seriously, "I stopped." Then she studied art for several years with one Ivan Serpa, "a concretionist." One day in his studio "the idea came to me just like that: to be a primitive."

How did Professor Serpa take that?" I asked. "He whistled with joy!"

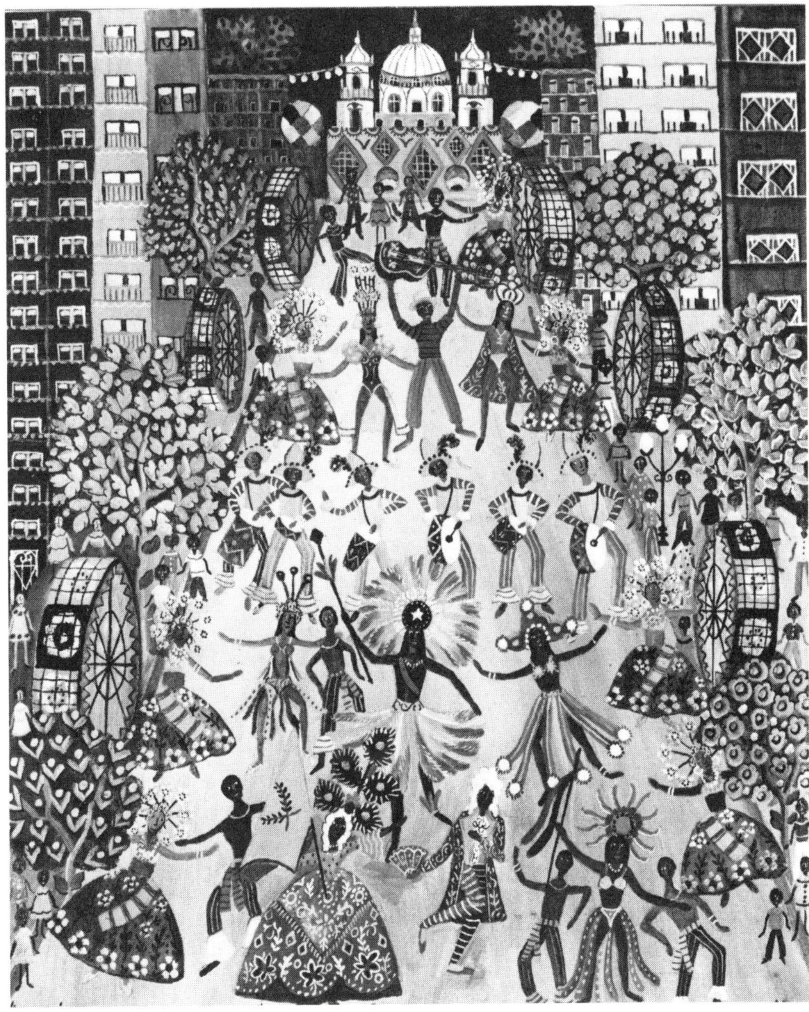

Figure 48. Samba School in the Rio Carnival. By Rosina Becker do Valle. Private Collection.

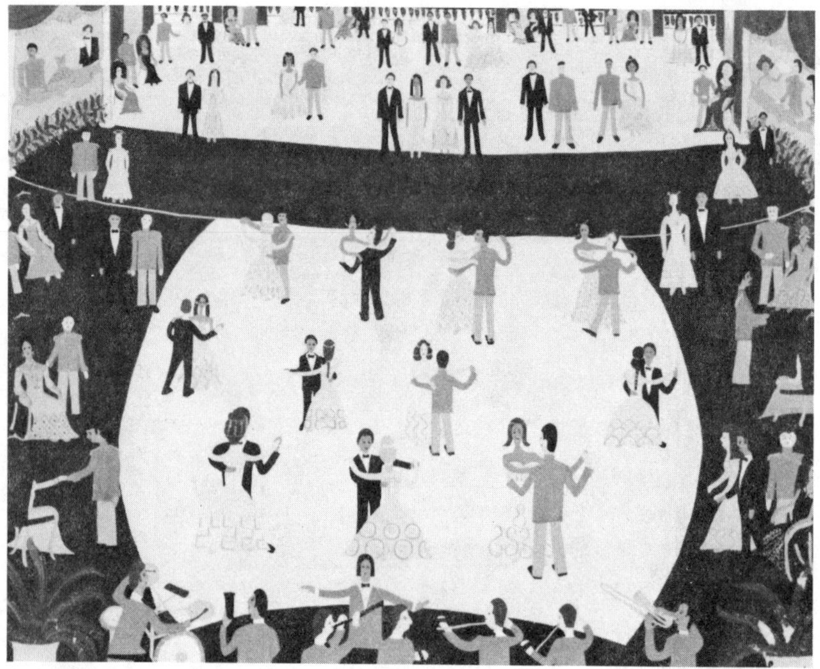

Figure 49. Formal Ball. By Maria Lacerda. Private Collection. Photo: Marilyn Bridges.

On her studio wall Rosina had written several mottos. "A journey a thousand miles long begins with one little step"—Confucius. "Man must live, not just exist"—Jack London. And her own cautionary advice: "It's more sensible to try not to fall into an abyss than to try to survive afterwards." The décor of her living room features two mobiles, one of insects, one of birds. Her favorite popular artist is Elza, Gerson de Souza's former wife. Rosina keeps several pictures going at once, moving from one to another. She worked two weeks on the only finished one, a "Virgin and Child with Three Angels" and was asking 8000 *cruzeiros* ($1,000) for it.

Maria Lacerda might have seen in São Paulo's Museum of Modern Art the picture of a soccer match in a crowded stadium by her friend Rosina. Her own soccer matches, formal balloon ascensions and crowded streetcars are no less impressive and quite different since the emphasis is on the figures and their movements rather than on spectacles seen distantly with the emphasis on pattern. (Figure 49)

Maria Lacerda was a *marchande de peintures,* who decided quite late in life to stop wheeling and dealing in the trite fare of the international school and paint pictures celebrating the life around her in Rio. This decision was made one day when her husband left her and she said to herself: "Who am I? Nothing but an entrepreneur in other men's creations—and creations that I have begun to despise!" That was in 1966. She sat down and painted "Cosmé, Damião e Doum," a fable involving the Twins of *candomblé* which she had heard from her "spiritual mother," the famous *Mãe de santo,* Menininha da Gantois, in Salvador. There she had grown up, though born in Paraîba in 1924.

I asked her why none of her other pictures dealt with *candomblé*. The cult, she reminded me frowns upon interpretations of its mysteries through works of art. She has sold some of her pictures for modest prices, but she supports herself and her children in high style—an apartment on Copacabana beach, flights to Paris and New York—by dealing in antiques and colonial paintings.

NEUTON AND WILMA

Neuton Freitas Andrade, who was born in Timburi in São Paulo state in 1938, started painting in 1959 at the suggestion of a friend, Américo Modañez. He and his friend soon began to sell their pictures at the Mini-Gallery established by Allan Fisher, Cultural Affairs Officer in the American Cosulate in São Paulo. This lively gallery became an outlet during the late 1960s and early 1970s for many of the popular artists of the city. It was there

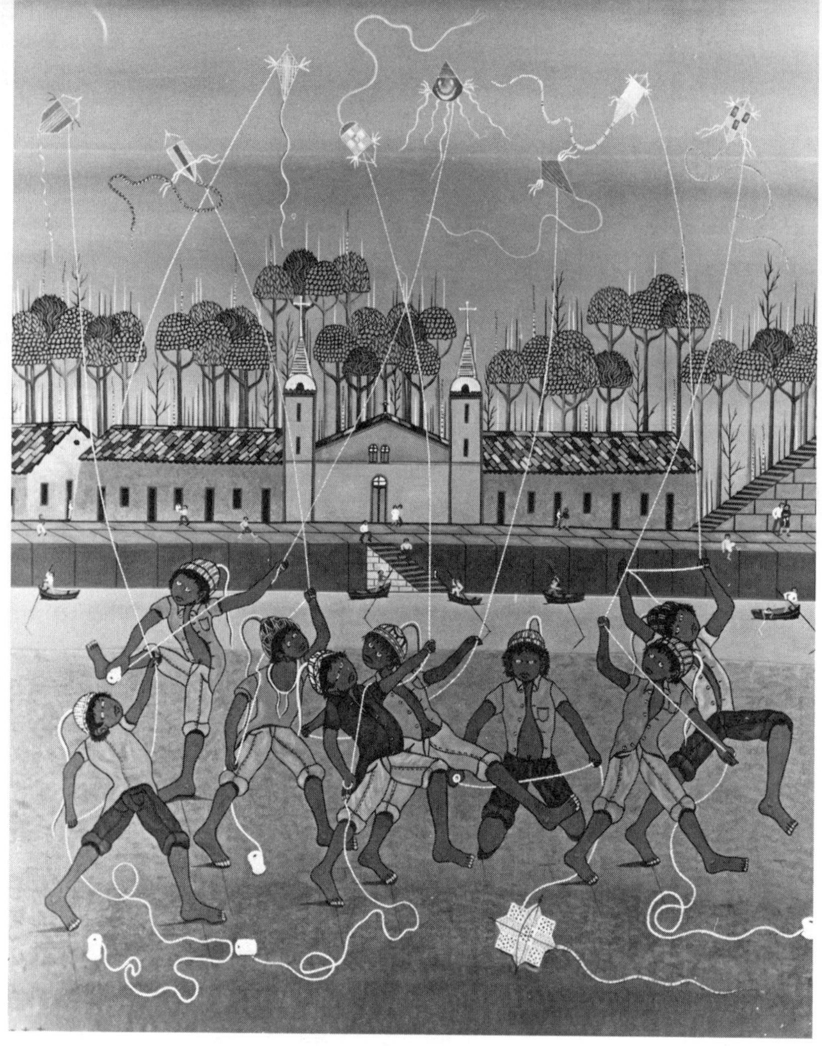

Figure 50. Kite Flyers. By Neuton Freitas de Andrade. Private Collection, São Paulo.

in 1971 that I saw and bought Neuton's picture of a Judas scarecrow being poked and buffeted by participators in a popular New Year's Day village fiesta.

This painting, like all of Neuton's at that time, was characterized by a dark mysterious atmosphere, the illumination seeming to come mainly from the figures' *eyes,* which glow incandescently. As late as 1974, in such a picture as "Kite Flyers" (Figure 50) Neuton sustains their image, but his recent pictures, sold mainly at his stand in the so-called "Hippie Fair" in the Praça Republica on Sundays, seem to have been painted hastily.

Wilma, another young artist of the Praça Republica who got her start at the Mini-Gallery, specializes in scenes of *candomblé* in which the participants are veiled (Color Plate 4B). An aspect of *candomblé* comforting to many city dwellers, is the freedom from anxieties that comes from yielding one's personality to the possessive spirit.

FRANCISO V. DA SILVA

Another self-taught artist of great early promise was Francisco V. da Silva, a sailor in the Brazilian Navy who now lives at Casa Grande on the outskirts of Rio de Janeiro. He began by painting bordellos, remembered from ports-of-call up and down the coast, with a gusto truly Breughelian, though lacking the Flemish master's tragic grandeur. The humor with which the

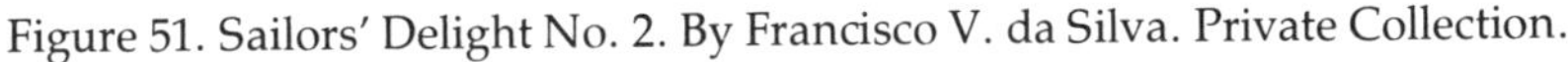
Figure 51. Sailors' Delight No. 2. By Francisco V. da Silva. Private Collection.

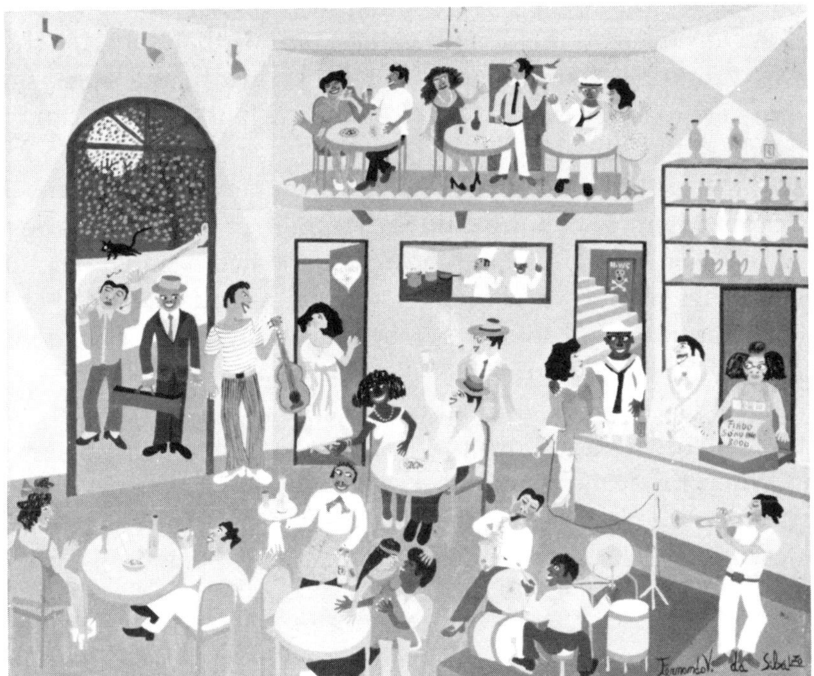

Brazilian artist conveys these scenes is matched only by José Antônio da Silva—to whom Fernando is not related, and whose pictures he had not seen. The differences between them, perhaps, is that José Antônio is a poet, Fernando a reporter-cartoonist. In his two pictures entitled "Sailors' Delight" (Color Plate 4C, Figure 51) a sociologist of the future would learn more about what life was like in such a *boîte de nuit* (including the functional art on display) than he would from a hundred photographs. The sociologist would also have a hard time deciding whether the tarts or their clients were having the most fun.

ISABEL DE JESÚS

The great Nicaraguan popular painter Asîlia Guillén would have spent her life embroidering pillowcases if an art lover hadn't urged her one day to transfer her little figures to canvas. Isabel de Jesús' canvases are like embroidery and she, too, might never have painted had she not met Iraçema Arditi, the sophisticated naive, now living in Paris, whose fluid landscapes filled with pretty birds and flowers enraptured her.

When Iraçema's influence became so strong that Isabel felt she was losing her very identity, she broke away, and began to remember, as in a dream, the real birds, fish and flowers of her childhood in Minas Gerais.

She was born there, in Cabo Verdo, but moved to the state of Paraná when very young. The Sisters there prepared her to be a nun, but just before taking the vows, she had a similar fear of losing her identity, and became a nurse instead. These experiences of imminent loss of personality, escape, and metamorphosis are reflected in a series of early pictures painted after she had settled in São Paulo: human figures with faces of birds or beasts, entwined in flowering tendrils.

When I first met her, Isabel was living in the district of the metropolis called Paraîso, the window of her apartment giving a downhill view of gardens and tiled roofs truly "paradisal." Shy,

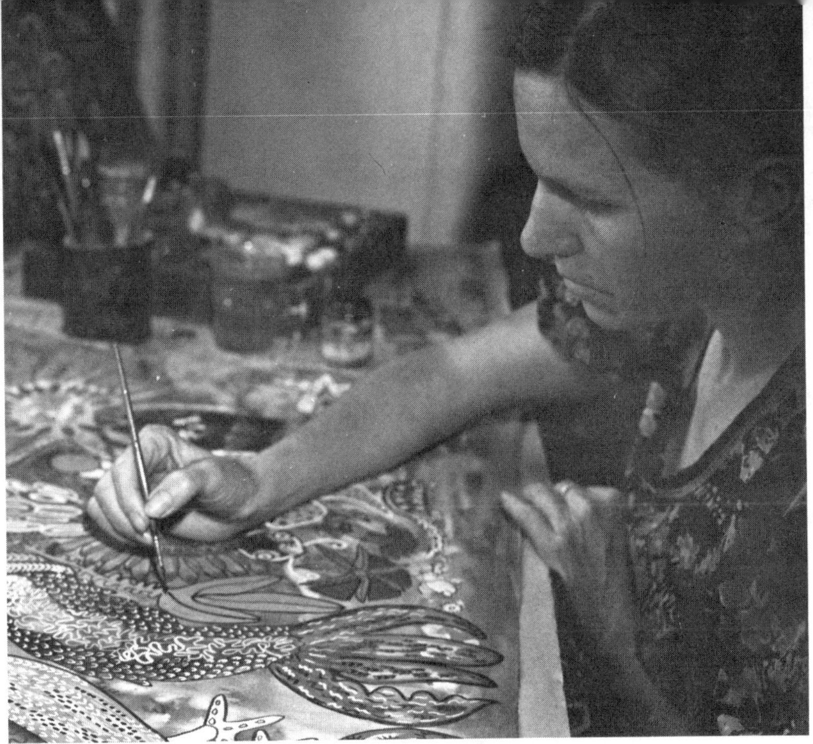

Figure 52. Isabel de Jesús at work in her studio, São Paulo. Photo: Manu Sassoonian.

dedicated, intense, she draws so continually and compulsively that while we were talking to her (Figure 52) her brush never stopped adding leaves to a vine and delicately veining them. Even a window-pane sprouted plants, and the lid of her paint-box was a corona of daisies.

The pitfall of such dreamlike doodling is that pictures tend to become little more than decoration. The patterning of doves, flowers and stars in such a picture as "Virgin Holding a Necklace" (Figure 53) is a little too symmetrical and crowded, saved from being no more than a religious chromo by Isabel's sensitive use of color.

IVONALDO AND IAPONI

More ambitious artists of the São Paulo school of popular art are Ivonaldo and Iaponi Araujo.

Ivonaldo was born in Caruarú in Pernambuco and lived for a

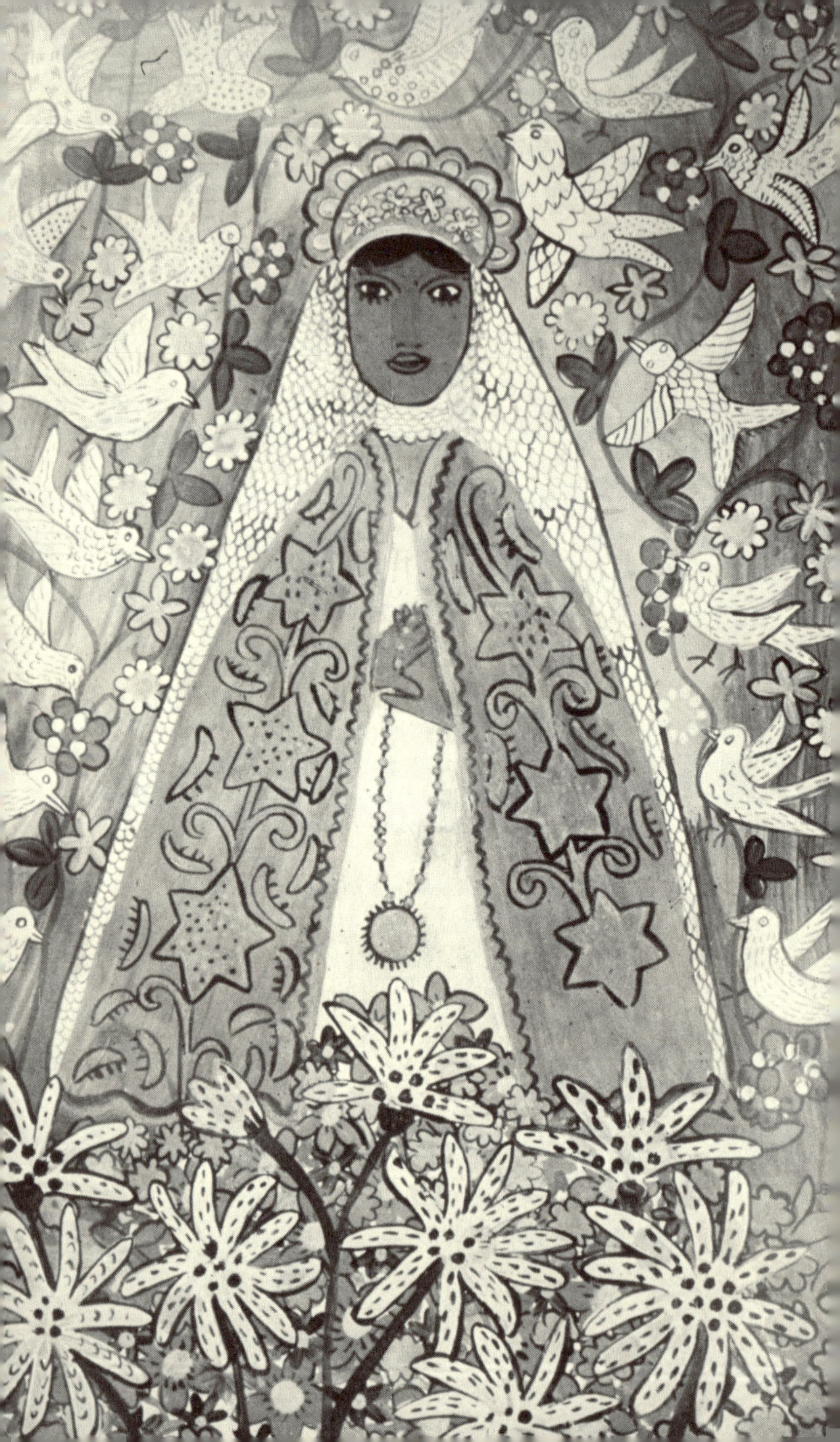

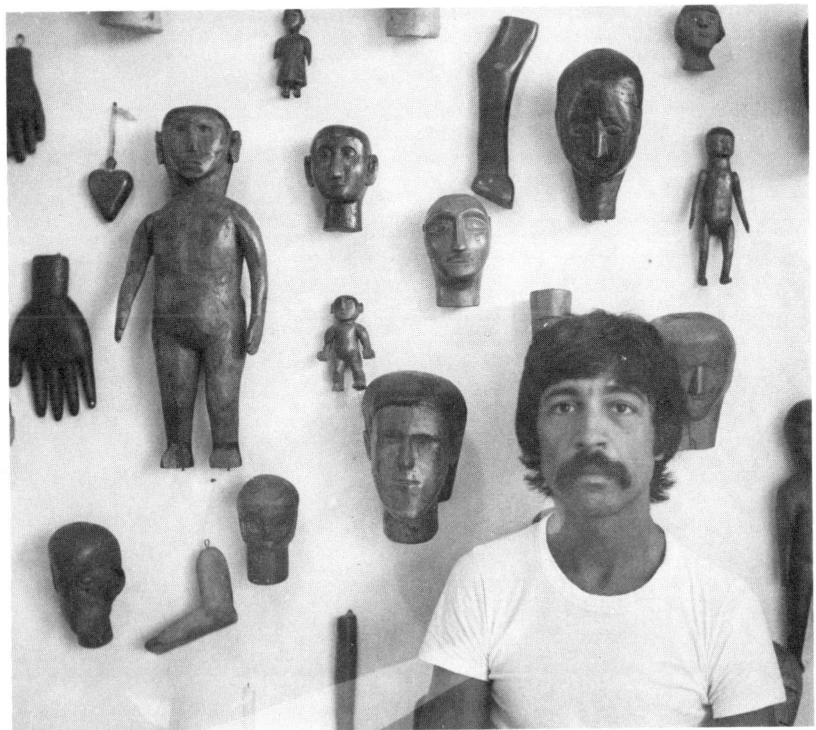

Figure 54. Ivonaldo and his collection of ex-votos, São Paulo. Photo: William Negron.

time in the state of Ceará where he collected several dozen splendid *ex votos* of carved wood which hang from one wall of his São Paulo studio and against which Bill Negron photographed him (Figure 54). His other walls are covered with a fine collection of the popular artists' pictures: Maria Auxiliadora, Waldomiro, Gerson de Souza, Ze Inácio, José Antônio da Silva, and many others. He brought with him from Caruarú one of Vitalino's last ceramics. And he also collects old sewing machines, stoppered glass bottles, and religious crêches.

This eclectic taste is reflected in Ivonaldo's own large pictures of grotesque figures and horned animals, painted in predominant browns and blacks. The draftsmanship is bold and the compositions are striking, somewhat in Waldomiro's manner but without that artist's intense motivation.

Figure 53. (opposite) Virgin Holding a Necklace. By Isabel de Jesús. Collection: Author. PhotoG Manu Sassoonian.

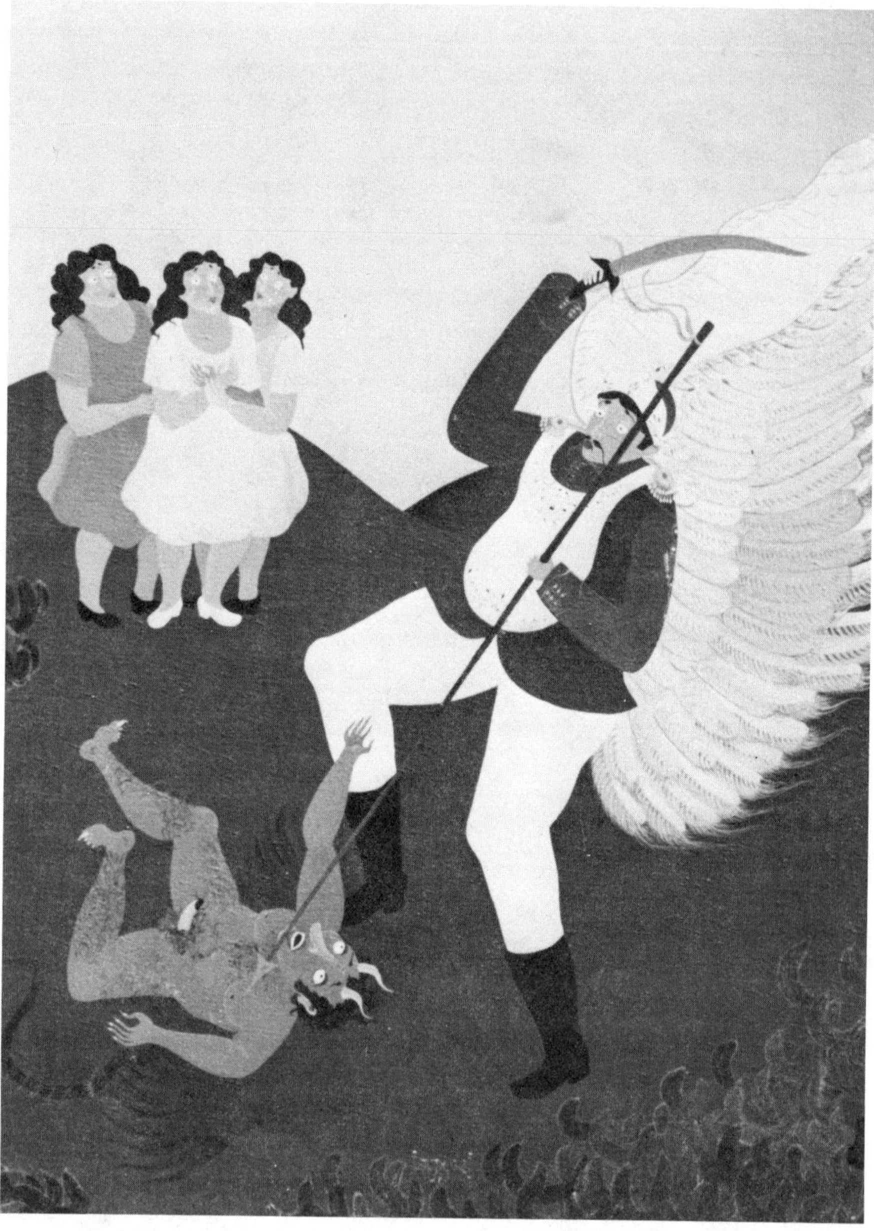

Figure 55. St. George Exorcizing a Demon. By Iaponi. Collection: Author. Photo: Marilyn Bridges.

Iaponi de Araujo Soares also comes from the Northeast. Born of *caboclo* parents in the city of São Vicente in Rio Grande do Norte, he now lives in Rio but paints the legends of his birth-state almost exclusively. These legends are painted romantically, for their pictorial exoticism, never compulsively as Waldomiro paints them. For example, in his picture of St. George spearing a dragon who has been threatening (or inhabiting?) three damsels on a hillside (Figure 55), one remembers the saint's gorgeous white wings and the monster's bristles; the expressions of the menaced maidens register neither fear nor relief. In another picture, widely reproduced, of a girl with streaming black hair lying asleep on her back in a shallow jungle pool, the effect is even more romantic, tinged this time by a suspicion of lurking danger, like a "still" from *Rashomon*. Did Iaponi receive his name because of some trace of Japanese ancestry, or was he given it because he painted such pictures?

MARIA AUXILIADORA SILVA

It was a terrible loss to Brazilian popular art when Maria Auxiliadora Silva died of cancer in 1974. She was a young woman (Figure 56) and had been painting only four or five years. I saw her work for the first time in 1971 in the anteroom of a São Paulo collector who was contemplating adding a popular artist to his collection. I introduced her to the Mini-Gallery. Allan Fisher and others began to sell her pictures at good prices.

She had had from the outset a very personal style. Perhaps because she had been a housemaid, she painted interiors minutely observed (Color Plate 3D)—and nature beyond the windows luxuriating in its freedom.

Perhaps from this circumstance of her servitude, or possibly with an intuition that her life as an artist would be short, she sought some means of giving this joyful discovery of a world an added dimension. And in so doing she invented something entirely new in painting: an undercoat of paste and other sub-

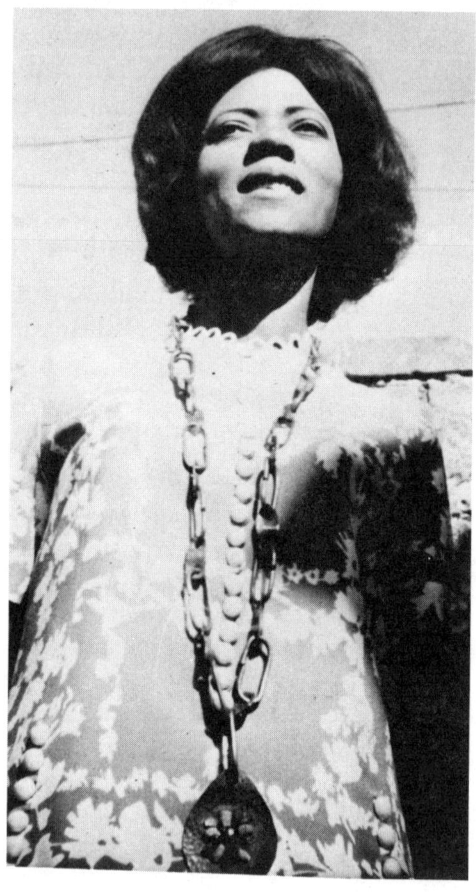

Figure 56A. Maria Auxiliadora Silva. Photo courtesy of Crisaldo Morais.

Figure 56. (opposite) Dancer in *Candomblé*. By Maria Auxiliadora Silva. Private Collection, São Paulo.

stances that would enable portions of the pigment to rise above the picture-plane in low relief. Thus, for example, the breasts of her women swell, features are slightly sculptured, and flowers emerge from leaves as though visibly blooming. In the hands of a lesser artist, such a device might be obtrusive, even gimmicky, but in Maria Auxiliadora's freshly discovered world, things bulge naturally because they have to.

The dancer in one of her last pictures (Figure 56) is a masterly triumph of impassioned movement over densely patterned detail.

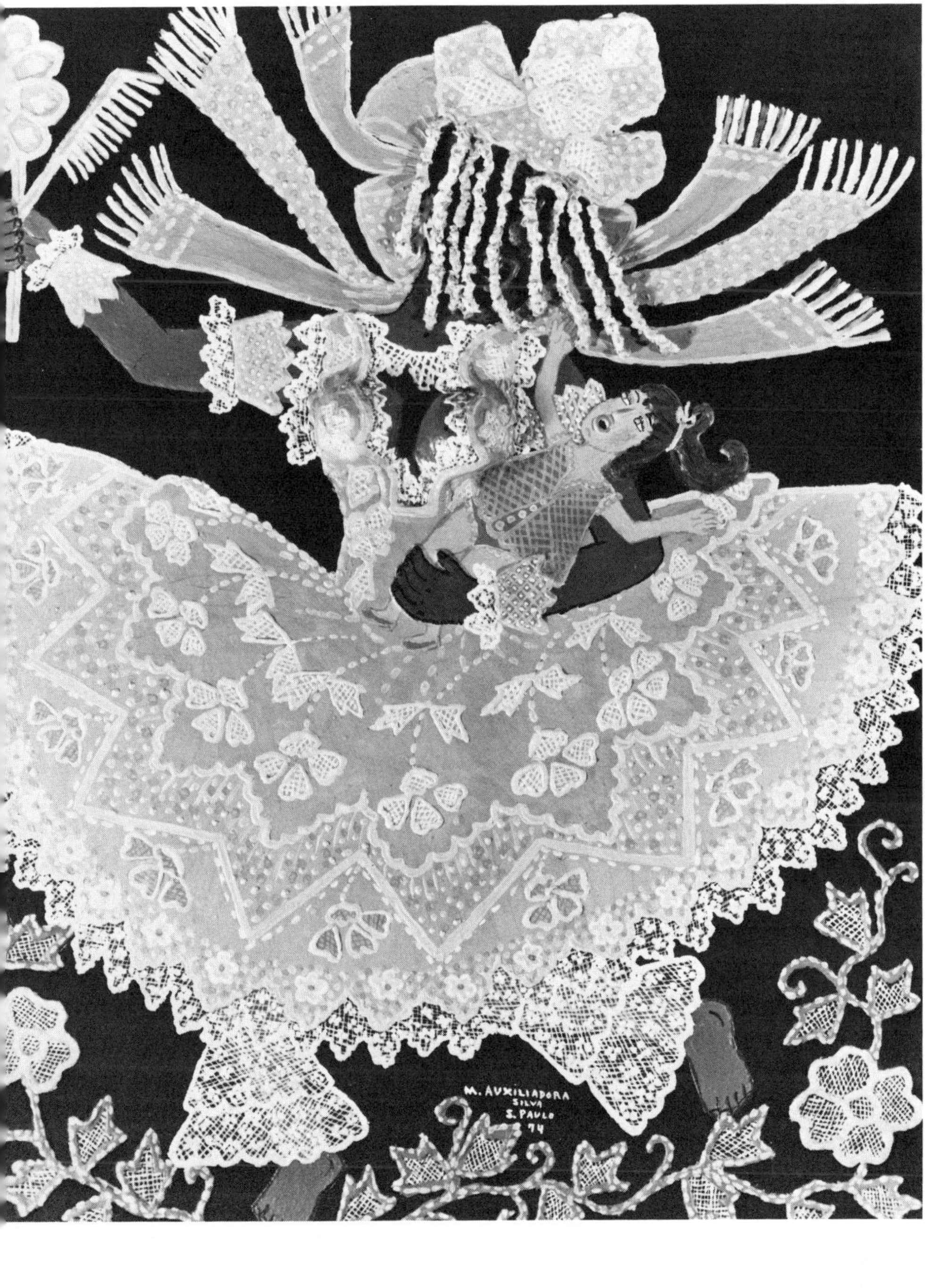

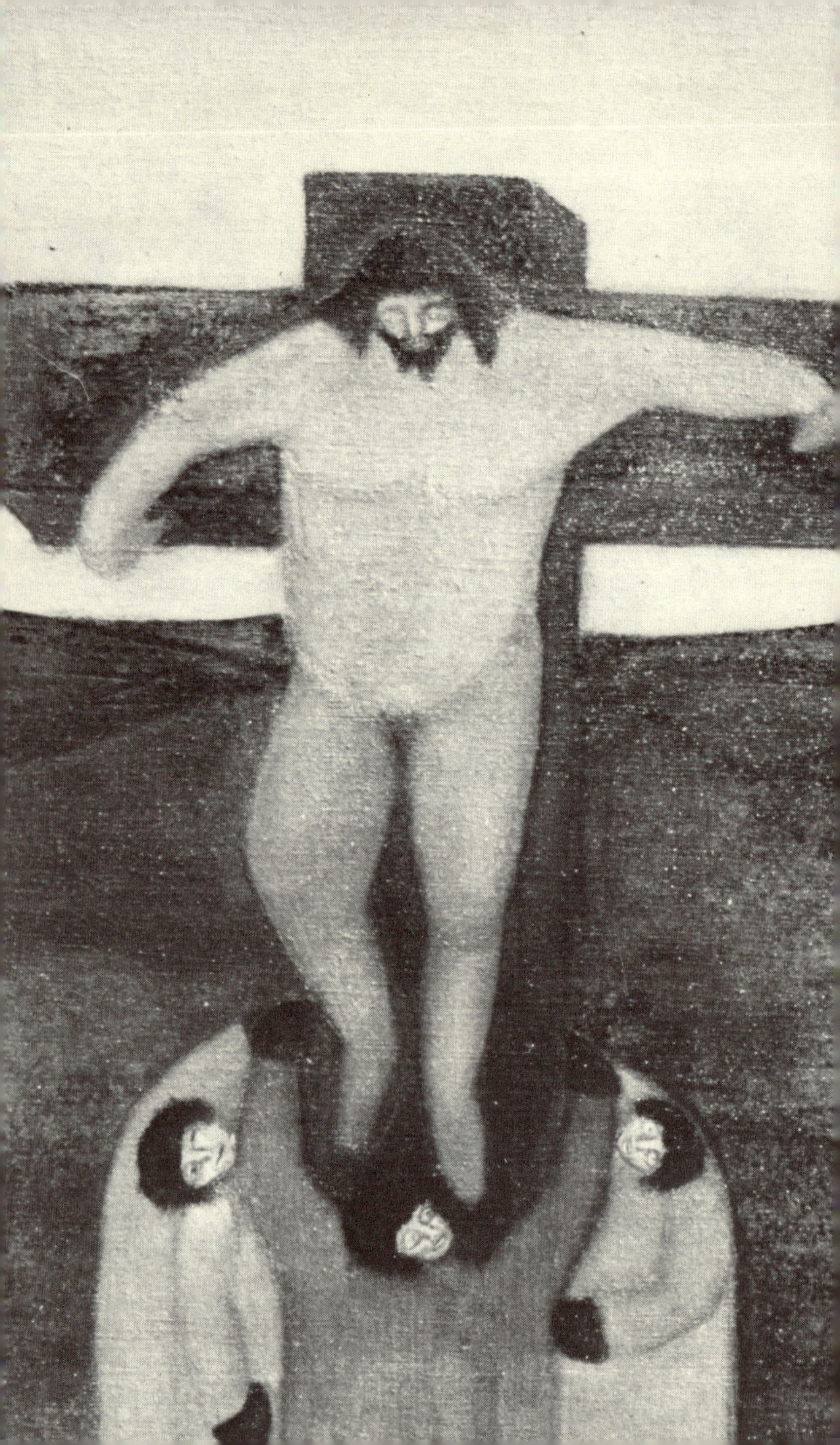

GERSON DE SOUZA

On black trapezes
your acrobats
without necks,
elbows, knees,
balance on pot
upside down.
The unstable stance
of a white clown
is your salute
to all we've got.

In the blue night
like a black bat
your freaked-out Jesus
hangs to stay:
tired of waiting
centuries for sinners
to shape up,
he droops supine,
bulging, blue,
and gone to fat.[1]

The key of A
flat minor, best
presents
those gents
in red brocade
or Tyrian purple:
epauletted,
silver fretted,
mitred like
the armless one
with sceptered eye:
Silenus Rex.[2]

[1]Figure 58.

[2]Color Plate 4D.

gure 58. Blue Crucifixion. By Gerson de Souza. Collection: Author. Photo: larilyn Bridges.

Your view of sex
what guilt discloses!
what monstrous depths
of childhood fears!
The padlocked penis
ever nears
the flaming mouth
and ever fails;
the one with wings
erectly fierce
will never reach
in golden noons
Leblon's hot beach,
but only pierce
the seamless seas,
the skins of moons.

Armed with a number
(out of date),
a mug-shot
out of which your grin
and wall-eyed look
through steel-rimmed soot
defied pursuit,
I ran you down,
From flat to flat
that you had fled
I got the gate,
till finally at
your place of work
they said:
"The postal clerk
will soon be in."

Back from your rounds
of sorting mail,
like some blind gnome
whose out-of-bounds
will be a fall
through inner space,
you hugged the wall.
You made no sounds.
As soft as braille
I followed you
to Home Sweet Home.[1]

I found you in.
(I found you out)
Euphoria
of urban shack
with lolling Lolas,
flies and phlegm,
nippled Mabs
and dogs with scabs
dirty dishes,
rotten fishes,
Coca Colas...
but at your back
La Glória:[2]
the hurt of art,
the heart of dirt.

[1]Figure 59.

[2]Gem of the Brazilian Baroque, visible from Gerson's window.

Gerson, your art's
no idle fiction,
no swivelled trope
of contradiction.
Whirled
and swirled,
surreal, expended,
yet always poised
imperially,
your Knave of Hearts.
and cross-eyed tarts
are all up-ended...

This is our world:
its laws perverse
enough to fleece
the naked poor
and coat the rich;
enough to hex
the once-pure air;
a world to curse:
with laundered money,
cheated sex—
yet strangely new
and wildly funny,
and tinged with hope
as seen by you.

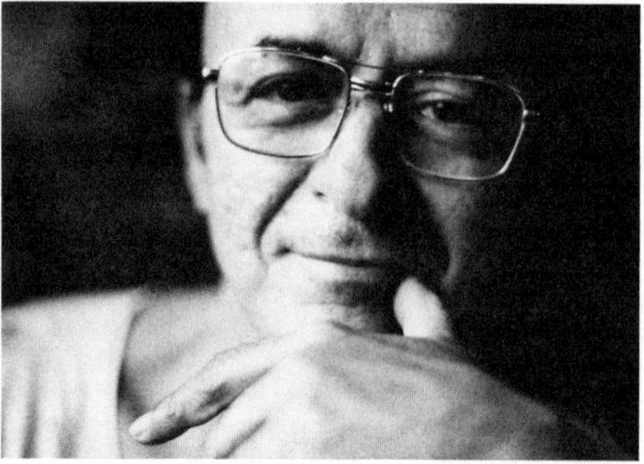

Figure 59. Gerson de Souza at his Rio apartment. Photo: William Negron.

Appendix I

A LETTER FROM GERSON

After completing this book, with its final chapter on Gerson de Souza, I received the following letter from the artist, answering questions I had put to him about "The King and Eye," his erotic paintings, and the general direction of his work. The letter is of such interest that I offer herewith the relevant parts in their entirety:

Rio de Janeiro
January 6, 1976

Dear friend Selden:

...Yes, I received *The Brazil Traveler* and thank you for it. My plans for the future? To try to improve my painting, to convey better what I feel. To endure the pressures of this Violent World which leaves me scared and lost, and where I keep asking myself: What is it all for? I'm always depressed, although it may not show, feeling an enormous sadness in my soul. Life is beautiful, Nature works correctly, everything is made of beauty and love yet people are running around without knowing where to or why.

Everything I paint has a tinge of eroticism. Having sex is like breathing and should not be considered an immorality to be suppressed; I believe that many physical tensions and even some of those of the soul result from prohibiting the practice of sex.

A "king" knows everything. He can have people killed. The people kneel at his feet, but he is a prisoner, a solitary being surrounded by people who take care of his life, try his food, watch his bedroom. He does not have the right to love whom he wants. He has no right to privacy. This "king" of mine, however, is a plain man, a man who feels and sees the beauties and mysteries of the world. He is a poet, an artist, a writer, a teacher of all the intelligent and ignored human being who dream of a better world by have to keep silent, mutilated in their creativity since the days of the cave dwellers. The crown of my "king" is symbolic, all dreams since he is humble and great at the same time. His inner world gives him everything, since he sees everything, creates everything, with the music he desires, the colors and flavors he wants; suffering only from the convention that forbids him to talk and live naturally.

Concerning my favorite painters, I would rather not express any opinion lest I omit the many I don't know. Every painter has good intentions, although artists are by nature difficult people, tempermental like all those who create from inside themselves, trying to become better and more sensitive, working with soul, heart and brain 24 hours a day.

I'm happy that the language barrier is not in the way of our friendship, for we are all together in this great Universe...with a big "abraço."

GERSON DE SOUZA

Appendix II

Extracts from the foreword *(The Great Sea of Being and the Arts of Instinct)* to the catalogue of a 1974 exhibition in Rio de Janeiro entitled "Instinct and Popular Creativity"

by Lélia Coelho Frota

The common trait of looking with condensation (even if it's approval) at so-called marginal art must be re-examined by us. We cannot insert this art in a compartment, rustic or picturesque, tragic and socially demanding, and then eye it as interested spectators. For these artists express, with language values of their own quite on a par with ours, an inner reality known to all of us but brought close to home with unfamiliar devices. Art for these artists is part of the flow of life, but conveyed by breathing naturally rather than striking an attitude. And they practise what we call art without ascribing to it, as we do, a quintessential holiness....

It is indispensable that the analyst of "innate art" document himself thoroughly about the artist himself in order to evaluate and explain his or her production....

Instead of living among imposed shapes, wouldn't it be preferable and more enriching to belong to a society where creativity can be achieved by everybody, at a personal level?

Carlos Drummond de Andrade on Heitor Dos Prazeres: "Without conflicts, without renouncing the best in his background, Heitor integrated in the urban, cosmopolitan culture of Rio, giving us in so doing an example of purity and authenticity."

The art of the "primitives" leads one to believe that the creative gesture may one day be extended to every man....

ACKNOWLEDGEMENTS

With few exceptions, those to whom the author owes most are mentioned on the title page, in the dedication and text of this book. And that includes, most especially, the artists.

Foremost among the exceptions are Rubens Ricupero, Cultural Officer at the Embassy of Brasil in Washington, without whose encouragement, advice and assistance, the book would never have been written; and Barbara Griggs of the Devin-Adair Company, who believed in it before it was written, and guided it skillfully through all its phases.

Most helpful during my five visits to Brazil were Barbara Starr Wolf in São Paulo and Lélia Coelho Frota and Eliane Lage in Rio.

Also in São Paulo: Carlos von Schmid, Isabel de Castro Silveira, Irené Felman, Alan Fisher, Carson and Ellen Geld, Eleonora Budniok, Richard and Jane Hayes, Carlos Pinto, Gilsa Gosslar, Esmeraldo Tarquinio, Crisaldo Morais; in Rio: Iván Semelis, Juscelino Kubitschek, Marc Berkowits, Roberto Pontuál, Lacy de Rego Barros, Augusto Rodriguez; in Belo Horizonte: João Uchõa Camarão, Lúcia Machado de Almeida; in Tiradentes, Minas Gerais: Ana Maria Parsons and John Somers; in Ouro Prêto: Lilli Correia de Araujo; in Salvador da Bahia: Jorge Amado, Vinícius de Moraes, Jesús García, Nelson Cerqueira, Frances Switt, Clyde and Laís Morgan; and in Recife: Silvia Martins, Roberto Mota, Rich Brown and Gilberto Freyre.

To Helga Ancona, Brazilian-born, I owe a special debt of gratitude for her help with translations from the Portuguese.